HALF A PAIR OF PEOPLE

Patricia Huth

Same Author Publishing 2022

ISBN 978-1-3999-1911-1

The Moving Finger writes; and having writ

Moves on: nor all thy Piety nor Wit

Shall lure it back to cancel half a line

Nor all thy Tears wash out a word of it.

Omar Khayyam

Dear Jane

with very best wishes
and thanks for giving me
the confidence to continue
with this memoir.

Patricia Hulte
June 9th, 2022

To Francis with love and thanks

Contents

Chapter 1

Introduction

My first memory, aged five, was of a large white house with green shutters and a big garden. It had long creepy passages and enormous rooms pretty bare of furniture, and I always thought it was haunted. My father at that time was working as an actor and film producer at Pine Wood studios. He left early every morning, a chauffeur picked him up and dropped him back in the evening. Most of my early childhood my mother was absent. She had met a diplomat on the train from Reading to London and went off to live with him in Paris. She stayed at the George V Hotel.

Dad's girlfriend at the time was Margaret Lockwood a well-known film star whom I hated. When we were out in the garden she would find a piece of long wheatgrass, wind it in my hair and pull it.

We had various members of staff in this house, a butler called Welfare, and a cook called Mrs Mason. Mrs Mason had two children much the same age as my sister and I but we were not allowed to play with them my mother said when she was there. And we had darling nanny. Agnes Ellen Turner. Nanny was really my mother. I certainly think of her as such, she loved me and she was always safely there. She wrote to me at school and sent me toffees and books by Georgette Heyer. She was my first true love.

I remember Welfare, the butler, who polished things all day. He seemed to live in a cupboard and wore a green beige apron which came right down to the floor. There was always something to do, an abundance of silver ornaments for the dining room table and beautiful crystal glasses to be cleaned. I think his day started about six o'clock in the morning and I never saw him leave the cupboard.

I was sent to my first boarding school, Guildsborough Lodge, at the age of seven where I was very unhappy. Then I went to numerous other boarding schools including a convent in Paris. The convent made Dotheboys Hall from Dickens seem luxurious. I was in a dormitory of 26, a nun at each end of the row. All these places were pretty horrific until I was sent to Heathfield, in Ascot. This famous school was the Alma Mata of many well-known women including Princess Alexandra and Edwina Sandys - Sir Winston Churchill's granddaughter. She became a good friend of mine. Most of the girl's parents had titles, quite a few had titles of their own. My Irish grandmother paid for me to go there so that I could meet and make friends with girls from aristocratic homes. Which I did.

In 1957 I became a debutante, and I write about that at some length later on in the story. Suffice to say the whole procedure was a failure, not because I had hated it, because I did, but no one had proposed marriage to me. I was, as it were, on the shelf. At 17.

I married at 21 a public-school boy and went to live in a large manor house in the New Forest. And I lived a rich, grand and spoilt life. I had a part-time cook and two dailies, plus a gardener. My husband organized everything and I had little idea of how anything practical worked. I didn't pay the bills or call any workman who might be needed. Nor did I know how the *other half lived.*

My great friend, Fiona, Lady Montagu of Beaulieu, who lived at Palace House close to Ipley Manor where I lived, and I, often talked of how good it would be to be free, to be single again. I went to some incredible dinner parties in Palace House where I met many celebrities of the day. For instance, Tommy Steele, who was very nice and friendly and Diana Dors plus her two lovers, often visited. She was very lively and great fun. The butler brought round *pot* after dinner and I tried it once. For me it made everything much brighter but I wouldn't ever try it again. I smoked cigarettes which, at that time, was what I liked. Subsequently, of course, lung cancer was diagnosed.

But with all the material things anyone could want I wasn't happy. I had a fast car, jewellery and a mink coat, and I should have been happy but I wasn't. I read somewhere that Princess Diana said she had everything and nothing which I totally relate to, because without the one thing that I think brings happiness is being loved and having someone to love.

My husband was away in London most of the week and I felt lonely and unloved. My children went to boarding school and the house felt empty when they had gone. When I made my getaway, in a somewhat frail state of health and mind, I faced not only the prospect of complete and unaccustomed solitude, but also, I had to learn about very basic tasks that up until then my husband had dealt with. Living alone, though the prospect may be daunting, can be a state you learn to delight in. It needs self-discipline, imagination, a stock of resources and, if possible, help from a few friends. The process of adjustment is full of unseen hazards, mysteries, disappointments and rewards: but it is negotiable. I would like to think these small tales of my own journey through the maze might give some encouragement to others who are bent on setting forth in the hope of finding the answers too.

So, after much thought and agonizing I decided that I had to leave and start again, on my own. There had to be more to life than this. It was a very difficult decision as I had little or no money but knew that we only have one life and mine had to be as good as I could make it.

And I left for Oxford.

Chapter 2

The Start of the Single Life

August 24th, 1981 was the memorable day I moved into my own house to start the single life. During my days of married life, in an unruly house in Hampshire, I had often imagined the kind of house I would like for myself one day. Now at last, unbelievably, here it was – a small, terraced house in Oxford full of strange silence and future potential.

I have always loved small Victorian houses. My beloved nanny, Agnes Ellen Turner, lived in one in Canterbury. There were nine members of her family, three rooms in the house. Unfortunately, I never saw inside it, but imagined what it would have looked like from my voracious reading of Victorian novels. I saw the familiar kitchen from *Sons and Lovers* where Paul Morel and his mother used to sit; Anna Tellwright's back parlour with its bentwood rocking chair and an engraving of 'The Light of the World 'over the mantelpiece and the small black fireplaces as discussed in various Dickens' novels.

These would, I knew, radiate a cosy, settled, all-embracing feeling coming not from luxury, but from love. There would be the smell of beeswax, sparkling blackened grates, and according to season, jars of wild flowers, bluebells or dog roses picked on Sunday rambles. In front of the fire on winter afternoons there would be buttered muffins, honey, and numerous cups of lemon tea. The street itself would be tidy, uniform, and predictable, like

Coronation Street, with small front gardens behind spruce hedges. That image was my Utopia, and I recognized it immediately in the small, dilapidated house I found in East Oxford. The outside resembled a squat, with flaking paint and dirt-grimed walls; the inside was filthy. Masses of newspapers and circulars everywhere, windows you couldn't see through, electricity meters in every room and graffiti on the walls. The garden was full of old bedsteads, curious pieces of rusty ironware, empty beer cans and empty bottles. However, in the hall a shaft of sunlight shone through the dusty haze. I glimpsed Anna, Paul and Mrs Morel, and Fanny Price (before she went to Mansfield Park) flitting about; and I fancied I smelt the beeswax. At that moment I fell in love with it, made an offer that afternoon which was accepted and settled in the day after. A good choice, as it has been the most constant and supportive lover I have ever had; always warm, always welcoming, always loving and always there.

Plumbers, electricians, and painters during the intervening four months worked long and hard on improvements making the house habitable. Four small downstairs rooms were made into one large sitting room, and a large kitchen with a door to the garden. Both dry and wet rot had spread happily and freely everywhere and needed a stay of execution; a hot water tank had to be installed and radiators fixed to the walls. Cupboards were fitted and the house rewired. (Little reference is made by Victorian novelists to cupboard space. I suppose it lacks romance as a subject, nevertheless I always wonder where the characters put their clothes since nineteenth century street houses appear to have been built without them. Ditto modern houses).

The day I moved in there were no carpets, no curtains, no electricity, and the telephone had yet to be connected. However, until the builders, who incidentally had become my first friends in Oxford left that evening, I was euphoric. All day I boiled saucepans of water to make cups of tea and I made jokes. The unreality of dreaming of a house of my own had become a reality. Unbelievably, this small part of the universe belonged to me, somewhere to root myself. Ken and Eddy left at 5 o'clock wishing me goodnight and hoping that I would enjoy the first evening alone in house. But, as with most anticipated events that fall short of expectations, this was no exception.

The much sought-after silence in the house seemed oppressive rather than peaceful. Putting away China, hanging the pictures, and generally straightening the muddle, lost its appeal as a solitary pursuit. The excitement of being solitary, of being free (that freedom so sought after, so much discussed, so often) and the single life for which I had fought and now attained, diminished, it seemed on acquaintance. I thought of the Schopenhauer quote: "He who does not enjoy solitude does not love freedom", and decided that solitude equalling freedom would be an acquired taste, arrived at in time, with much planning, effort and thought. As it was, I had forgotten to buy any food. So hungry, cold, and feeling less courageous than I expected, I burst into tears. Until that evening I did not realize exactly what it would be like to be totally alone: something which is perhaps not possible to know until experienced. In the midst of noisy families women dream of endless peace and quiet on their own, sure that they would be entirely happy in isolation. But in truth they might be no such thing. An hour or two maybe.... But real solitude, though aspired to by many, is in practice only really enjoyed by a few.

Anyway, I made pots of tea, and cheered myself up reading *Persuasion* by candlelight. Jane Austin, was, after all, single, and she seemed to have managed all right. (My reliable friends out of books are as one would wish, human friends to be, constant, predictable, and peaceful. Peaceful, perhaps, because they are constant and predictable). That first night I went to bed with mixed feelings, many apprehensions and a constantly re-occurring thought. Had I been extremely foolish in my desire for independence? In the weeks that followed, before I decided what I was going to do with my life, I discovered some very important facts about single living. Planning a structured day, and sticking to the plan, was vital. The radio provided my mealtimes admirably;

I had breakfast with lovely Terry Wogan until he misguidedly left his large adoring audience to prostitute himself on the television. I had lunch with Robin Day to acquaint myself briefly with news of the outside world, and at 7.07pm had supper with the Archers who have now become an integral part of my life. Perfect entertainment at the end of the day, Shula's love life or lack of it, Nigel Pargetter's misdemeanours, Brian's affair with Caroline, Eddy Grundy touching up the girl sent to Grange Farm by the Council for experience as a nursery nurse (but not that experience) and every evening I silently thanked God that

8

the most irritating woman ever invented, Peggy Archer, was no relation of mine.

Many mock the Archers. They see the series as unrealistic in the modern world. But man is not supposed to be able to bear too much reality, and life in Ambridge can provide a continuity missing from real life, a sense of security and safety brought about by a proper order of things. And, of course, the radio provides the sound of a human voice. A necessity to solitary people, who buy canaries, sticklebacks, cats or whatever as an excuse to converse out loud with something. I bought a large brown Teddy bear and called him Aristotle to share my bed, but so far have baulked at talking to him, although he would, I feel, understand as much or as little as the canary, stickleback, cat or whatever.

Administration of bills, coping with solicitors over the house purchase, trying to understand tax forms, sorting out money problems and generally being totally responsible for myself was, at first, extremely frightening. I had had no part in these activities as a married woman and I was quite convinced that I would be completely unable to tackle them. But I did. And I could. It came as a great surprise to me just how capable I was, having been under the impression, while married that I was almost moronic. I did the desk work in the mornings. Necessary fresh air was taken daily, after lunch. Oxford is traditionally a city full of bicycle riders. (I think many of them bicycle with an image of someone else in mind. Either a girl at a secretarial college trying to resemble a student or a student trying to resemble an academic. Or a North Oxford housewife trying out her Greenham Common outfit). Anyway, I hate bicycles, and maniacal cyclists. So, I tried a new venture, walking, which proved both beneficial as exercise, and uplifting.

It is a magical experience exploring the diversities of Oxford on foot. Watching the canal boats at Donnington Bridge, visiting the beautiful colleges, or walking through the water meadows and stopping on the way back in a bookshop, was a perfect way to spend the afternoon. In the evening after supper, I learnt to enjoy the peace. It is, I know, corny to elaborate on the process of 'knowing thyself'. Newly single people, intent on finding their own 'space', whatever that means, can bore on about it interminably. But as Socrates, Alexander Pope and Herman Hess strongly recommended the idea of knowing oneself, and as I greatly respect their judgement, that is precisely what I tried to do.

More from circumstance than from conscious planning I discovered my real hates. Violence, aggression, confusion, and noise (endemic in our society) are abhorrent to me. Finding this out was important on practical grounds. For instance, those mouth-watering jobs I saw when I was job-hunting – advertising for personal assistants or secretaries to help employers build empires, or to meet interesting/exciting top people, and/or the ability to leave the country at a moment's notice, all share the same snag: 'to be able to work under pressure.'. This means noise, confusion, aggression and probably some kind of violence to achieve the first three.

I am quite slow. Slow at everything. So, if I found a job which meant working under pressure, by about Wednesday of my first I would probably be needing the outpatients' department in the nearest asylum. So would my boss. I regrettably found myself to be sensitive where others are less so. I take offence where none is intended. This is extremely boring, but a fact that I seem unable to change. But discovering my frailties was a help in choosing the kind of life and job most suitable to my temperament. Depression, despair, and misery swept over me quite frequently in the early months. It struck around the hour of the dawn chorus. Sleep was impossible. Eventually, however, I did find some good ways of combating it. Thought control at night was essential; simply not allowing your thoughts to stray into depressing areas. I made literary problems for myself to work out. I pondered upon what Miss Haversham would have done with her life if she had not decided to spend it in one dark and cobwebby room. Or, had she lived now, would Lady Bartram have risen from her sofa to raise money for the Conservative Party, or NSPCC or rather, in her case, for the RSPCA? That sort of thing. Sewing is soothing at 3.15am and with the World Service and a cup of tea quite an enjoyable way of spending the night. My sewing abilities are non-existent, but I made an attempt to master easy patchwork; now tablecloths and several cushions stitched in the early hours.

My sister gave me some tapes of Peggy Ashcroft reading four Katherine Mansfield short stories. These were wonderfully sleep-inducing. Early on I learnt far the most crucial and important lesson. I could not doubt my decision to change my life. Much careful thought, much agony had been gone through to arrive at that decision. Having found the nerve or courage to swop a protected married life for a solitary single one in which there were a mass of new worries besides quite a difference in material things, I had to keep believing I had done the right thing. There could be absolutely no looking back. Nietzsche said: "What does not destroy me, makes me stronger". I began to understand the wisdom of his words. I was not destroyed. I grew stronger every day.

Chapter 3

Expectations – Discoveries – Satisfactions

People are disappointing and expectations of them (unlike Pip's) should not be great. Indeed, the way to afford oneself some nice surprises is if one begins with no expectations at all. Without being unduly pessimistic, just realistic, I came to expect nothing from anyone one or anything. If something rewarding happened, that was a bonus. For instance, I met a man at a publishing party given by my sister for her new book launch. He was very tall, elegant, and articulate. I discussed books with him, elaborating on my dislike of the contemporary novel.

"Anita Brookner is wonderful" he said. "I'll send you her latest three novels and guarantee that you will enjoy them". Well, he did, and I did. But it was an exception. People promise to introduce me to a wonderful single man they know. Or they promise to telephone, or return a borrowed book, or send a postcard from faraway places, or just to lend their calculator to ease the pain of sorting out tax returns. But they seldom, if ever, do. They say they will come to lunch or to dinner, but rarely come on time and, frequently, do not turn up at all. Once I accepted that this is quite normal behaviour, that people's word was not their bond, as it were, and I stopped expecting it to be, life became much simpler. It is a frailty of human nature that man's actions often fall far short of his intentions, and to accept that fact helps to keep one's calm.

The conditioning of women when I was young was that they should be subservient and submissive. They should have no identity of their own and voice no opinions. Such a condition is of little help to those who wish to survive a single life. My inability to say 'no' resulted in a dotty amount of hard work. In the early months people I barely knew wanting a bed in Oxford, stayed in my house – friends of friends who I had not the courage to discourage. I looked after other people's children, had dogs to stay, and even joined both the Labour Party and Conservative Party as a consequence of this inability to say no. I am basically wet. Rather than argue or have confrontations I acquiesce to achieve peace. But the irony is that wetness creates more problems, not less. The Bible says "the meek shall inherit the earth" which might be true long-term, but in the short-term it is not so. The strong, determined, positive and decisive win every time. I had to learn to be more assertive, to be tougher.

An essential early survival lesson is to say what you mean straight away, and stick to it. If you don't want to walk the neighbour's dog, look after her children while she goes to see an afternoon performance of Val Doonican, or fetch someone's brother from London Airport at 3am, say you won't and don't.

A new, important, and interesting discovery was how vulnerable I had become. Felicity a friend, who had been single between marriages, had given me some advice. "You can't have a man to tea", she said, "when you are single". How ridiculous, what an exaggeration, I thought. But she was right. My first encounter with this peculiar hazard was when I was looking for someone to help me with the garden. He was to remove bedsteads and beer cans, and generally prepare the ground for planting. I checked the postcards in the local post office and saw a likely candidate by the name of Phil. Do anything, it said on the postcard. And anything was what he meant, as it turned out. To arrange times and terms I told him to meet me at the house at 2 o'clock one afternoon. He turned up at 3 o'clock after a few fortifying beers at the Eagle and Child. He had a white emaciated face, long straggly unwashed black hair, was aged about 30 but looked older. He wore a large leather belt with several chains around the waist, cowboy boots, tight jeans, and a denim jacket. Not much like Mr McGregor, I thought. We sat at the kitchen table.

"Do you know much about gardens?" I asked him. There was a silence. "No" he said, "I know nothing about gardens. I am a student of the philosophy of life." He then asked me what my husband did and I told him I was separated and living alone. Immediately an anticipatory light shone in his eyes. He looked at me with a new interest.

"As a matter of fact," he said, "I don't feel like working this afternoon. Why don't you and I go somewhere more comfortable?" The thought of being anywhere comfortable with Phil made me laugh. When I had dissuaded him from the idea he laughed too, and said it was always worth a try, you never knew. And then he left to further philosophize on life. The garden stayed as it was.

Some summer mornings I talked to a male neighbour over our adjoining fence. A bachelor of 38, who worked at the Oxford University Press. He liked skiing holidays and growing tomatoes, he said. One evening I answered a knock on the door, and there he was. Ever polite (in those days) I asked him in because he said there was some matter he wished to discuss with me. Something to do with finding him a cleaning lady. He thought I might know of one. I made cups of coffee. After ten minutes he looked at his watch.

"Time for bed, do you think" he said. "What do you mean, time for bed?" I said, incredulous. "Well, it's obvious" he said, "you are on your own, I am on my own, sex can be a good way to pass the evening...".

The next close encounter was a fellow magistrate. I had been a magistrate for twelve years, during which time I had come to the conclusion that male magistrates were some of the most sexually frustrated men I had ever met, anywhere. So, I should have known better. After sitting in Court one cold snowy December afternoon, I boarded a bus for home in the company of this fellow on the Bench. We chatted as far as my destination and when I got out, he got out.

"Do you live far from here?" he asked, "I could do with a cup of tea." I should have remembered Felicity's warning. The magistrate settled himself in the sitting-room while I made the tea in the kitchen – thus revealing he was a male chauvinist pig as well as a sex maniac. I took the tea through on a tray and sat down opposite him. Suddenly, with loud yell and a mighty leap, as demonstrated by Robert Redford and Paul Newman hurtling into the cavern during the chase in *Butch Cassidy and the Sundance Kid*, he was on top of me, pinning me into the chair, shouting filthy suggestions. I disentangled myself and told him in two assertive words what to do. "Ah well" he said, "if that is how it is, and there is no sex to be had, I might as well go home." The tea was left as untouched as my garden.

From these unromantic scenes I learnt a vital lesson: my desirability was simply due to my availability. There was no point in flattering myself. The fact is that almost any woman, regardless of shape, size, or comeliness, is curiously attractive to any visiting heterosexual man. (Window cleaner and milkman jokes are not without foundation.) There is always the off-chance she will succumb. It seems from the man's point of view it is always worth trying. However, I make no judgements. Since the male of the species has been a hunter since evolution, perhaps there should be no blame attached to their attempts. I simply made a rule never to be alone in the house with a man – unless he was a trusted personal friend.

As a single woman I soon found myself thrust into another new category. Not only was I available, I was also, apparently, threatening. A threat, at least, to wives. Dinner invitations, as a separated over forty-year-old, came as frequently as Christmas during the year. I discovered why at the only one I went to. It was a pretty country house in an affluent conservative commuter village near Winchester. I had been asked for 7.45pm but arrived a little late having lost the way. The effect on me as I walked into the drawing-room was that I had mistakenly come upon an amateur dramatic group rehearsing one of Noel Coward's drawing-room farces. There was a large log fire ablaze, two Labradors asleep in front of it. Fruitwood and oak tables were dotted about, weighed down with family photographs in heavy silver frames. The sofas and chairs were covered in birds of paradise chintz. In the corner the grand piano staggered under copies of Harpers and Queen, Tatlers and expensive unread coffee-table books. The men were wearing dinner jackets, the women long dresses. I was introduced to them; four married couples and a polo-playing lord without his wife. She was at a health farm, he said, but later in the evening he revealed they were not 'getting on'. (Perhaps, I thought, she was 'somewhere more comfortable' with her butler, gardener, gamekeeper, or some lesser mortal with more vitality and sex appeal than her fat dull husband.) Whisky, vodka, and gin and tonics were being liberally splashed about to help lubricate the incredibly boring conversation.

If I had to describe the sort of man, I really detest it would be the loud, arrogant, self-opinionated, insensitive churl who brays like Bottom and whose education invariably took place at a 'top Public School'. At dinner, one such man, an Old Etonian in commerce, floor polishing to be precise, was on my right. As a woman and therefore expected to feed the lines, I asked him what he did. He told me at great length. He bored on about the types of brushes needed for different floor surfaces, about his profit margins, his charges, which kind of parquet floor needed which kind of polish and so on. In fact lots of jolly interesting tips, had I been contemplating floor polishing as a career. However, even he had exhausted the topic by the time we were halfway through the main course.

"So, what does your husband do?" he then said. (This type of man doesn't imagine that women do anything worth talking about). I told him I was separated. Thereupon he shook and bellowed, winked, nudged, in a most peculiar manner. When his agitation had subsided he asked me where I lived, and I told him. Puce in the face, his eyes rolling, he shouted: "Then I'll come up to Oxford one day and do you a favour with some of my best brushes." Ho ho.... His wife, from the other end of the table, had been watching me with a malicious look in her eye. She must have heard the last sentence, indeed none of the guests could have missed it. In a shrill voice, she enquired why I was "luring her husband to Oxford" and not to worry, she tittered, she knew all about single women. Frustrated, of course, trapping unsuspecting innocent husbands.

The man on the other side of me was of Russian aristocratic descent, he said. He was also a Turgenev fan. (What a surprise that someone had actually read a book at this gathering.) We discussed some of Turgenev's books and he mentioned one I didn't know.

"I heard you say that you live in Oxford. I'll be up there next week and could bring it round" he said. Untruthfully I told him I would be away for a month of two. I am constantly amazed by the continuation of the curious habit by some British upper-class males who stay in the dining room after dinner to drink port and swap fishing/hunting/shooting tales, or tell each other hilarious crude jokes. They can still laugh uproariously at the mere mention of tits, bums, knickers, or the Karma Sutra. Sex for them is still a furtive pleasure. They still believe that 'nice' girls have sex for procreation (the close-your-eyes-and-think-of-England variety) but those incredible orgies can only be with 'tarts'.

Their complete inability to give their wives any sort of pleasure from their loutish lovemaking is probably why the gamekeeper *et al* have such a success with the upper-class ladies. The ladies, meanwhile, go upstairs to 'powder their noses'. Then ready for the fray, they gather in the drawing room again to wait for the 'boys' to appear.

There was a heavy frost pervading the air when I returned to the drawing room that evening. Four of the women were sitting side by side on the sofa as though lined up to one of Kitchener's stands. The men returned, now crimson from the port, smoking large Havana cigars. The wives stood up, took aim, and fired. Time to go home they said as one, and clutching onto their marital rights, as it were, muttering to the hostess about their early starts, they hastened away. Motoring home, I though how strange that those men, being so hateful, could bring about such jealously and anxiety in their spouses' breasts. The wives worked, I suppose, on the premise that any man is better than no man, and if that was all they had then they were all for keeping it.

But despite the many occasions I experienced the unpopularity of being single, the altered tempo of life exposed me to new satisfactions. Feminists would be appalled, I am sure, at the very idea that housework could be either interesting, fulfilling, therapeutic or something to look forward to. I found it all these things and more. The pleasures of ironing, for instance are immense. The smoothing iron should I think be known as the 'soothing iron'. Ironing restores more tranquillity to the soul in half an hour than any tranquilizers. Listening to a play on Radio 4, whilst watching piles of fresh laundry grow on the kitchen table is, to me, a perfect way to spend the afternoon. Then there is furniture polishing, hoovering, dusting, sewing and hanging up the washing all to enjoy. I feel like Mrs Tiggywinkle (and much the same shape) proudly bustling around my house. Finally, satisfaction of the garden. I had always thought garden enthusiasts even more tedious than Royal Family enthusiasts, squash or golf enthusiasts, car enthusiasts or people belonging to the Ecology Party. But I was wrong. The small patch outside my kitchen that is the garden had become an imaginable delight. Although gardens are something of a mystery for beginners, and all the things to learn are not a little daunting, the results are worth the struggle. I am easily confused about compost heaps, fertilizers, annuals, evergreens, bulbs, seeds, cutting back and pruning, but gardens are forgiving and anxious to please. Perhaps the aura of mystery and necessary esoteric knowledge is perpetuated by proud garden owners showing off their ability to know and remember the plants and shrubs by their Latin names, and then telling frightening tales of 6 o'clock risings to put in the three- or four-hours necessary work each day to keep the garden pristine. I simply bought various seeds in Tesco that looked pleasing and scattered them about. The pansies did not appear, but everything else came up. Which proves that arbitrary scattering with little or no skill involved will produce flowers.

And, as my attempts at teaching myself to propagate new life advanced a little each week, so did the growth of my own renaissance.

Chapter 4

New Challenges – Different Standards

Is there anything new to be said about cigarette smoking either for or against? I think not. You smoke because you want to, or you smoke because you are addicted, and your addiction beats your willpower to discontinue. Or you do not smoke, never have, and think it is disgusting. For me, as from the age of 15, I ventured out into all weathers, I sought out unused lavatories and I loitered in dark passages or wherever else I could light up without discovery, and the smoking habit caught fire. It continued to blaze brightly for the next twenty-five years, and when I came to Oxford I was smoking thirty-five cigarettes a day. Discourses on 'how I gave up smoking' are boring to everyone. If you don't smoke, then you cannot enjoy the fuss and agony of giving up, and if you do smoke, have tried to give up and haven't succeeded, it is incredibly irritating to hear those who have managed, talking self-righteously about how clever they are. Listening to Miriam Stoppard on the radio one day, that glamorous television/doctor personality twittering on about how well she felt now that she no longer smoked and how 'we could all do it' if we were determined and so on, I felt like killing her, not emulating her.

Suffice it to say, therefore, that with great difficulty I did stop smoking. However, I believe that once a smoker always a faintly reluctant non-smoker, and my constant dread is being, for any length of time, with people who smoke. After a week with them I would be back smoking myself. So, I try to keep away from smoking people and smoking places. The result of not smoking did not seem to be immediately beneficial. Indeed, the opposite was true. Not only was I irritable and bad tempered, but I became fatter and fatter. I put on two stone in about 6 months. Fair and forty go together, I know, but it was difficult to discern whether it was the middle-age spread, or the lack of nicotine to speed the metabolism, that was causing the embonpoint. Or both. Living alone had presented new problems of what, with no fuss, could I cook for myself. Cooking a Sunday joint for one was ridiculous, expensive, and unnecessary. Making a stew and having to eat it for four consecutive days in order to finish it was a kind of self-inflicted culinary punishment. It reminded me of the Christmas turkey. Delicious on the 25th, good on the 26th, less so on the 27th and horrible thereafter. Puddings fared no better. Even a small apple crumble, reheated on day two, is fairly unappetizing, so it joined the uneaten stew in the dustbin.

Good food is not on my list of essential priorities for happy living. I seldom notice what I am eating – indeed I am sometimes surprised to see an empty beans tin in the sink when I have no recollection of eating them whatsoever. It has always been a puzzle to me just how much discussion takes place about the relative recipes, restaurants, wines and so on, as if they were a serious and important part of life. Eating is generally supposed, I believe, to be the optimum pleasure in middle age when the pleasures of sex abate. Since my enjoyment of eating exciting or rich food is non-existent I can only hope that the pleasure of sex will ever continue. Life, otherwise, promises to be fairly dull.

But, obviously, gaining so much weight, I was eating the wrong food. Finally, I went to see someone in the menopause department at the Oxford Hospital. It might, I thought hopefully, be hormone imbalance, and I could find something for it. The doctor I saw was young and aggressive. She asked me lots of questions, mostly about how much I drank.

"Do you drink a lot?" she said. Doctors always ask this question in a voice suggesting that they never touch drink and that they suspect that you are an alcoholic.

"How much is a lot?" I asked. "Do you mean do I drink two bottles of gin a day or two glasses of sherry after church on Sunday?" She did not find me amusing. Finally, she wrote something on a piece of paper. She had written one word on it: o-b-e-s-e. OBESE! Horrible thoughts flew round my head. Obesity is serious. It implies several things – none of them good. Greed, lack of self-control, lack of pride, lack of intelligence, and obviously, lack of willpower, were just the first few. But the dietician was very nice. She explained that human beings were designed for a lifestyle, after evolution, as hoers of land and drawers or water. We needed then, with the fresh air, exercise and long hours toiling, the benefit of three large meals a day. This obviously no longer generally applies. Certainly, I should eat very little because I do very little. Two or three apples, a little fish or chicken, All Bran and two slices of wholemeal bread, 'washed down' with lashings of tea (with skimmed milk) or water, is about

25

all I can eat each day if I want to stay slim. (My nanny would have been horrified. She taught my sister and I that three meals a day were essential for our wellbeing).

Now, years later, I have the gist of slimming. It is for every day of the year, every year, ad infinitum. It is hard work and boring, and whether it is worth it is debatable. I try to keep to the prescribed diet but sometimes rebel and buy delicious homemade fudge, in a pretty packet, and eat it all in one go. And I love it. I know now when I am fatter than I wish to be, and take steps. I have accepted that my weight problem is a life battle, and that it will never go away. When I become overweight, by my standards, I go on the Cambridge diet for a week or two, which is painless and very effective. I like having a chocolate drink for breakfast, turkey soup for lunch and mushroom soup for dinner and know that I am losing two pounds a day with no effort. So that is what I do. It works, and it is cheap.

At the beginning of the eighties, exercise became fashionable. Aerobics, jogging, running, squash, dance movement, yoga et al plus Jane Fonda telling us all to 'burn'. (I tried 'burning' one day, fell over backwards and could not walk for a fortnight). Strolling about through water meadows or walking in the wonderful Welsh mountains at my own unhurried pace is perfect exercise, it seems, for me. Violent activity gives me a headache, and I avoid it wherever possible. But, pressurized in my first year in Oxford, I felt reluctantly that I should emulate my fellows. I joined a class of enthusiastic ladies at an exercise class run in a health farm, advertised in the local paper. This was a serious mistake. The health farm, set in a luxurious private estate, was designed to give a feeling of ease and relaxation.

Thick, plain carpets in every room, bowls of expensive flower arrangements everywhere, and new copies of Good Housekeeping and Vogue lay on the waiting-room table. There was a suffocating richness in the very air, as if the place itself was preening its superiority.

The woman taking the class was straight out of Dallas, I imagine, or some such fantasy grown-up fairy-tale world. She had long silky blonde hair, long red nails, lots of make-up and a lovely figure clad in hundreds of pounds worth of leopard skin leotard, plus trimmings. The morning of my first class I had carefully chosen what to wear. An old pair of black tights, feet cut off, seemed appropriate: they would be taken for half a leotard. Plus, one of my daughter's T-shirts. This ensemble appeared to be perfectly adequate when I tried it on at home, but in the changing room (all pine louver doors) I saw it in a rather different light. The other members of class had brought in neat little Gucci changing bags, brilliant aquamarine, red, purple and peacock blue leotards (from Harrods, I gathered), with matching tops, and some strange garments called leg warmers (not articles of clothing I could immediately see a use for. We were not ballet dancers, were we?).

Looking around, I felt no empathy here and to say that I was the odd man out would be a great understatement. We trouped off to an exercise room with a parquet floor and William Morris chintz curtains. For the next hour, to the sounds of some classical music (Chopin would have been appalled at the antics his Mazurkas inspired) and some popular music, we bent and stretched, lay on the floor with our legs in the air, pointed our toes, danced on the spot, and generally asked our bodies to behave in an irregular manner. Mine rebelled against it all. At the end of the hour I escaped thankfully, my body indignant at such unwelcome exercise, my mind stupefied by the waste of time and money. A lovely walk over open fields with an abundance of fresh air, aesthetic views, and music from the wind 'listing where it bloweth' – my kind of exercise – was surely better for the body and soul than cavorting about in an expensive health farm.

Several months later, inspired by a friend who said that exercise in the form of free dance movement was sheer delight, I made one further attempt at communal exercise activity. The Church Hall, where the dance movement took place on a Tuesday evening, was very different from the Health Hall. It was cold and dirty with a worn-out air. There were no changing rooms and as far as I could tell, no lavatories. But here, at least, the other class members did not wear exotic leotards and where my cut-off tights and T-shirts were *de rigeur*. An indeterminate lady thumped out music from an old piano whilst another tried to bring some form of order into the class's dancing by shouting out things such as:

"Feet in, feet out, to the right, bend to the left, bend in, bend out, jump, and again.... "I never came to grips with it at all. It seemed that whilst listening for the next instructions, was behind with the previous one so that I was bending or jumping when everyone else was doing the opposite. I persevered for several weeks but there was no improvement in my timing, and although I quite enjoyed the dancing to describe it as 'sheer delight' was certainly overdoing it. I abandoned the struggle for coordination.

What I continued to struggle with, however, was with the acceptance of the fact that standards have to change in a single life if the sought-after peace is to be attained. Different standards and different values are inevitable, there is less time, less money, and less willingness to spend either on yourself or your friends. I found alcohol expensive and dangerous to keep in the house. Dangerous because drinking alone can lead to drinking too much, too often.

Having discovered this, I asked friends to bring their own vodka, gin, beer or whatever, which they did willingly, thereby saving me from expense and temptation. Dinner party invitations issued by me, translated, mean come to supper, early, for stew and apple crumble, instead of smoked salmon, rump steak and four vintage wines – the invitations of yesteryear. Nobody seems to mind; I have no complaints. Many a lively evening is spent over simple fare, drinking bottles of the Tesco equivalent of Sancerre. As for the washing up, it gets left. I used to be obsessive about washing up, it always had to be done as soon as the offending dirty crockery touched the draining board. Having always thought J Wesley's quote "Cleanliness is next to Godliness" is indisputable, I have since learnt that this is not so.

To be clean, yes; but to be obsessive about washing the body, washing the dishes or washing anything is absurd.

Manufacturers are constantly inventing new, ever more lethal 'cleaners'. For instance, detergents once designed to clean the lavatory pan are now guaranteed to take care of the inner cleanliness of the pipes as well. Our forebears did not hanker after pipe-inner-cleanliness, and nor should we. What the detergent does, probably, is to filter into the canals and waterways killing off plant life and poisoning the fish. Anyway, now I rule the washing up, it does not rule me. If I want to leave it overnight or for any length of time, I do.

The friends who come to visit want primarily to see me. If the house is full of fresh flowers (it is not usually), has clean towels in the bathroom, and I arrange for 'interesting' people to come to supper, that is a bonus, not a necessity. Friends want to relax, exchange news, gossip and grumble a bit, make jokes, and leave feeling better for their visit. Hostesses should give their guests their time and attention, otherwise, it's much nicer for them to go and stay at a hotel if they merely need a change. I do what I can. What is lacking in material comforts is forgiven (i.e., the mattresses in the spare room are lumpy, apparently). What I know I can provide is a place of refuge, in a peaceful house. I work at making it so. I like to think the peace my house bestows upon me will be of benefit to others, too. So far, in this sphere at least if my friends are to be believed, I seem to be having some success.

If I do have people to dinner and I don't very often, obviously I do spend more, but not much more. Homemade vegetable soup and garlic bread, curried chicken, and rice with baked courgettes perhaps plus carrots, followed by cheese and biscuits or fruit salad, is a favourite cheap menu for four people. It costs about £10. Normally guests are very generous and bring wine but I always buy a bottle or two costing about £2.50 each from Sainsbury's, who seem to have a large, good choice.

The only important conclusion I have come to about food is that For me, as in other matters where there is a large choice, I wish for less choice. The uncomplicated food I buy requires very little thought, and is a healthy diet. So much for food.

Among the Odd-Job Men: the importance of sifting the sharks from the saints

I have embraced the feminist movement with certain reservations. No doubt men are selfish and spoilt but, nevertheless, I like them. In a radio broadcast, Enoch Powell once said that men and women were built to complement each other, not to be identical, and that they should excel at different things. This fact has much revealed itself in a practical way since I have no 'houseman'.

I know nothing of electrical matters, Rawlplugs, or of manipulating Black and Deckers; neither can I dig strenuously or put up fences. I cannot paper walls or put in DIY double glazing, neither can I attach draught stoppers to the doors to any effect, or measure widths any degree of accuracy. Obviously, I could with time learn some of these skills. However, I am most inept at practical matters and not, I think, right temperamentally for precision. So, I needed an odd-job-man to help me.

There are plenty of them about. Postcards in the post office often tell of their whereabouts and their skills. Gardening, window cleaning, guttering, roof work, repairs, and other miscellaneous jobs are all on offer. Speaking from experience, I think 'who to trust' is a vital question when choosing someone to employ in your house with probably no references, and no personal recommendations. I am not naturally suspicious of anyone, especially if they are trying to work and are unemployed, but it is a wicked world, and it is important to be careful. If you live alone, consider what this man will know about you and your movements, your door and window locks – or the lack of them.

I employed a man, one Mr Talbot, who I found through the yellow pages, initially as a window cleaner, later as an odd-job-man. He was friendly and enthusiastic, but clumsy, unreliable, and an amazing liar. He had been an officer in the SAS he said, and told tales of spying in East Berlin. On one occasion he had been sent to quell an African uprising. Apparently, he had sat up trees in the jungle with his troops and, with great daring and accuracy, felled hundreds of warring tribesman. Later he had to leave the regiment on account of his teeth playing up. (Actually, I do not think he had ever left English shores). I list here just two of his many misdemeanours.

On his advice I bought a front door handle which he put on, taking off the existing rather pretty Victorian brass one. This new handle was too heavy for the lock and the pin in the middle broke under the weight. The inside handle then fell onto the hall floor when I was trying to use it one afternoon. Stuck outside, I had to pay £23 to an emergency locksmith to let me into my house. The Victorian handle was then put back in its original place on the front door. Mr Talbot, like Mr Toad, would say anything to have what he wanted, totally regardless of its truth. I had bought some tiles to put round the bath and asked him whether he was anything of a tiler. He had, apparently, been close to championship tiling – there was nothing he didn't know about it, he said. However, his skills deserted him with my bathroom tiles. He managed to break several, put two or three in the wrong place and stick the ones over the basin, upside down.

It seemed strange, thinking back, why I continued to employ him, knowing him to be almost useless. Perhaps it was his availability. Just when I was despairing of getting the Hoover going, or some such, there he was on the doorstep, enquiring about work. Stupidly I let him try again and he broke something else or committed a further misdemeanour. I am afraid that Mr Talbot is not at all unique in his inability to turn up on time or not at all, or to start jobs and not finish them. Or to pop down the local shop where his brother-in-law works, and buy you something which you do not require and haven't asked for. Fortunately, I have now, by chance, found a very good and reliable man, Mr Wood. But it took four years to find him and much wasted money, not to mention endless disappointments and risings of angry temperatures. At some time, it has to be decided whether odd-job-men are worth the stress they cause. Large firms are much more expensive and not always first rate, but at least with a company there are legal ways of retribution. There are none with the odd-job-man.

The inner peace of burglar prevention

All burglar prevention devices are money well spent. The house at night can creak, doors can slam, and nasty noises can waft up from the kitchen when the kitchen is supposed to be empty.

Alone, this creates high nervous tension, and I did not wish to die of a heart attack bought on by night nerves. My house was in the centre of the 'Oxford Rape Triangle' when three women, at separate addresses in my immediate neighbourhood, had their houses broken into and were then assaulted. In haste I had screw-locks put in all my windows, dead-locks on the outside doors, and special locks on all inside doors in the house. Unfortunately, it now looks like Fort Knox but at least I feel safe. In my view, whatever money is spent to ensure peace of mind cannot be too much and burglar devices should be a top priority.

I heard a woman who had started her own business talking on the radio about her experiences. The one certain thing she now knew, she said, was that she could trust nobody: that no one was trustworthy. If this were true, life would be very sad and gloomy, and I do not feel the same. But it is a sad truth that there are unprincipled people everywhere, especially in cities, on the lookout for easy money. And single women, particularly middle-aged women, unknowledgeable in worldly ways, are simple targ

Chapter 5

A Youthful Fantasy Realized

Until 1950 I lived near Windsor, so for many years of childhood was able to enjoy the famous Windsor pantomime. Each year I looked forward to it and was never disappointed. After the war, children had few treats so perhaps the ones we did have seemed extra memorable. It was at a production of Cinderella in 1947 – a vintage year – that I vowed I would one day perform in a pantomime myself.

Some thirty-five years later, a friend lunching with me in Oxford announced that the Chipping Norton Amateur Dramatic Society were auditioning for Dick Whittington the following evening. Here then, was my chance to fulfil the childish ambition to be in a pantomime. Chipping Norton is twenty-seven miles west from Oxford and this, in itself, should have been the best reason for not embarking on this particular venture. My twelve-year-old Renault 5 was temperamental enough in the warm months; in the winter it frequently could not, or would not, start at all. The heating worked erratically, petrol was expensive and my driving, never good, is at its worst in fog. Fog is known to descend nightly on the A34 Stratford Road making visibility practically impossible. Anyway, aged forty-two, I went.

The audition took place in a bungalow, the home of the director. I had some difficulty finding it when I eventually arrived, late, a collection of people were sitting on the floor already reading from scripts. I was given one and sat down. Glancing through the parts there didn't seem immediately to be one tailor-made for my potential talent. There were various female roles: the cat (I was too fat), Alice, the leading lady (I was too old and fat), Dick Whittington,(I was too old, too fat and there were too many lines to learn), and a variety of Arabian ladies, dancing girls and chorus girls none of which seemed entirely suitable. That left one possibility, the good fairy. I was given her lines to read and knew instinctively that the part of Fairy Silverchime would be offered to me. I deduced this from the lack of anyone else's apparent willingness, rather than for my obvious reading or acting ability. (I had the feeling the prospective cast is not supposed to state a preference for a certain part, but a keen bearded man from the VG stores particularly wanted to play King Rat. And said so. But he wasn't given it. It went to a more suitable candidate, a teacher from Banbury.

A week later, not having heard anything, and strictly keeping to the rules of "don't ring us, we'll ring you" the telephone rang and I was officially invited to play the pantomime fairy in the 1982 Chipping Norton production of Dick Whittington. Rehearsals took place at 7 o'clock on Tuesday evenings in various venues. Sometimes the assembly room in the local school, sometime in the Chipping Norton Theatre. (The Chipping Norton Theatre, incidentally, is absolutely delightful, remarkably pretty architecture, very small and full of atmosphere. It was built in 1888 as a Salvation Army citadel and opened as a theatre in 1975.)

Rehearsals in the early stages, when lines were read, were fun. An Amateur Dramatic Society has tremendous spirit and humour. Everyone was very friendly. There were lots of bad jokes, and a few arguments, but only in the same way that a united family argues, with love not aggression.

At 10 o'clock sharp when the director was beginning to lose control, we retired to the Crown and Cushion pub until closing time. Unlike the bar and beer at the Open University (which comes later), here, I was allowed to drink gin and tonic in peace, enjoying the theatre gossip. Past productions, future productions, costumes, who was going to paint the props this year, (it bloody well wasn't going to be whoever was talking at the time), speculations on Christmas weather, how many tickets would sell, or whether with the advent of videos, the pantomime would still be popular. And soon, I drove back to Oxford not minding the fog and cold, gin coursing through the veins, lulled into a false sense of security. At that stage having a part in a pantomime was all I had hoped for – my dreams – at last - come true.

The crunch came after Christmas. Rehearsals from then on were to be without scripts. The words had to be learnt. A vital factor that I hadn't 'known' about myself when I went for audition was that I was almost incapable of learning lines. The part of Fairy Silverchime was not a major role, and there were not more than three dozen lines, but I simply could not learn them. Perhaps, (excuses, I know) I felt faintly idiotic mouthing pantomime philosophy such as:

A triumph, evil's overthrown,

Once more doth good the victory own …. and so on.

Even for experienced good fairies or Dick Whittingtons, chatting to a pantomime cat on stage could, I suspect, present histrionic problems: for me it seemed impossible. I realized then that I had three major difficulties to overcome. First, learning the words. Secondly, saying them audibly when I had learnt them, and thirdly remembering from which side of the stage I had to enter, and when these changes had to take place. The fourth problem was that the amount of stress that all this worry produced meant the fairy's performance lowered the standard of the whole pantomime. Tiffany, my eldest daughter, who had studied drama for A levels, was staunch in her efforts to help me. She even tried to inspire in me a feeling for the part, but by now I had given up any thought of projecting the fairy's role. The only ambition I had left was not to dry up completely.

Agonies reached a climax at the first rehearsal on the actual stage. This was in the Town Hall. The Town Hall in Chipping Norton is built right in the middle of the town, an island with roads all round it. The stage entrance at the back of the building has very little room for congregating when not on stage. So that during the performances whilst waiting for entrances, I was frequently squashed for long periods between two teenage rats and several Arabian dancing girls. This uncomfortable and cold position was, however, preferable to returning to the dressing room. The dressing room was underneath the building, but in order to find it the High Street had to be negotiated. I did it once, in the fairy attire, mingling with afternoon shoppers. But you would need to be made of sterner stuff than I to do it twice.

For some reason at the first rehearsal the director decided that King Rat and Fairy Silverchime should run through their words first. My heart thumping in my chest, we went on stage. I heard King Rat snarling out his threatening lines, I looked down into the auditorium of empty chairs, and I knew that I wasn't going to be able to speak. And I couldn't. The blank mind, dry mouth, racing heart and sweating hands were to become very familiar companions during every rehearsal and throughout every single performance. Contrary to hearsay this condition never improved. My rendering of the ghastly rhyming couplets declined daily. My lack of conviction in their truth was the only thing that shone. Ron Bridger, who played Captain Cuttle, and Pete Webb, who played Idle Jack both had extremely long parts and complicated entrances, fights, songs to sing and dotty dances to perform. But it didn't seem to disturb them at all. If they did forget their lines they simply made up something appropriate and nobody seemed to mind or notice. Pete Webb was a very nice and amusing man who worked as a gamekeeper on a private estate. Before becoming a gamekeeper, he had been a drummer in a pop group. In the wings, to cheer me up and quieten the nerves he told me jokes about the groupies that followed them about. My favourite was:

Girl groupie after sex with a member of the band:

"Do you love me?"

Member of the band replies:

"Do I love you? I have just screwed you and bought you a packet of crisps – what more do you want?"

Wit, I know, is lacking from this story but it always made me laugh, perhaps for its sad reflection of the times, and a better understanding of why Mills and Boon novels sell so well. We had to make, borrow, or find our costumes. As my wardrobe contained nothing remotely suitable for a middle-aged fairy my sister produced a white lacy (second-hand) evening dress which fitted quite well, except that it was too long, which made walking a hazard. She also lent me some silver shoes. And I had a sparkling wand made out of tinfoil. Finally garnished in silver and white lace, under dim lights, I liked to think I made a tolerable fairy. (At one performance I was in the Ladies, during the interval, which we shared with the audience, when I heard a little girl say "look Mum, the fairy has just gone to the toilet." So, I convinced someone).

As the date for the first night approached, and my stage fright increased, tranquilizers seemed imperative. After some persuasion my doctor gave me Valium and I bought several bottles of wine from Tesco. The combination was bound to be effective, I thought. Indeed, at one performance, during the interval, having drunk more Liebfraumilch than was prudent, I dropped my left contact lens down the sink and couldn't find it. I had to continue in the second half with blurred vision. My performance was not improved by this, and God knows I didn't need any extra difficulties.

It was snowing hard on the morning of the opening night. Before I set off for Chipping Norton I tried to think of some credible reason as to why I shouldn't/couldn't or wouldn't go in order not to have to play Fairy Silverchime. However, after much deliberating, I felt my pathetic part was as much a total commitment as, say Dame Margot Fonteyn dancing in Swan Lake at a Royal Performance. The show would go on and I had to be in it. With the aid of Valium, wine, encouragement and resolution I went and staggered through that and every other night. The only bit I really enjoyed was the Finale. It was the relief I suppose, plus a similar feeling of patriotism and sentimentality aroused when singing Jerusalem with your school or last-night-at-the-proms enthusiasts. A united togetherness.

There was one funny moment. Peeping through the curtains one night I saw my brother-in-law, an Oxford don, and a friend of his, another Oxford don, entering into the spirit of the audience participation song "Bobbing up and down like this." They were waving their arms about, touching their heads and bending their knees as instructed by the Dame! I thought their students might be interested to observe the versatility of academics.

After the last performance we had the traditional party. Dancing, drinking and general merry-making took place. I had grown very fond of the cast over the months working together. They were an assorted bunch. Clerical workers, shop assistants, small shop-owners, farmworkers, housewives, a pigman who worked for a member of the Astor family (he was very effective as the Emperor of Morocco) and Peter the gamekeeper. I judged their moral lifestyle very high with husbands and wives respecting and loving each other. There was no hanky-panky here, although later I heard the pantomime cat had left her husband to settle with a tenor from the Chipping Norton Operatic Society. But this seemed to be an isolated case.

Amateur dramatics is a whole way of life. A sort of Dunkirk spirit runs through the members, helping each other in adversity and against the odds. It is like an extended family, with its own triumphs, intrigues, jealousies, failures, and successes. When the actors are not actually performing there are numerous other activities to occupy their time. Cricket matches, bring-and-buy mornings to raise money, barn dances, play-reading evenings, cooperative discussions on what next to perform, and always props to paint at the weekends before the pubs open and after they shut. It could be, and I am sure it is for some people, a total pre-occupation. And very nice too.

Their next production was to be Chekhov's Seagull. To go to watch it would be lovely, to be in it didn't bear contemplation. Once again it proved to me that fantasy and fact should not be confused. The nature of reality has been amply discussed by philosophers without them coming to any conclusion. But I know for me that while the fantasy of performing in a pantomime still remains wonderful, the reality, I remind myself every panto season, is not so.

Chapter 6

Mature-Student Days

Open University – Evening Classes – English Literature around the Kitchen Table

As a child, to please an eccentric grandmother who insisted on paying the school fees, I was sent to Heathfield, a boarding school near Eton. The priorities among the pupils in those days had little to do with learning, and I left after a few years of scant education with three O levels. Many years later I made some attempt to repair this state of affairs I joined evening classes, studied A level English and began a mammoth course of reading. But as a busy mother of three schoolchildren my latter-day studies were always forced to come second. So, it was not until I was alone and free in Oxford my opportunity came to make up for the lost years.

The Open University seems the obvious answer to my desire for some sort of intellectual achievement. It was started by Sir Harold Wilson in 1969 (and established by Royal Charter), with the admirable idea that countless poor people deprived of a good education, could, by entering the Open University obtain a degree. No qualifications are necessary, only a real desire for knowledge. Large measures of enthusiasm and stamina are necessary to face the six years of hard work needed to be awarded a degree, plus, two years more for an Honours Degree. It is possible to reduce the years by working on two courses simultaneously, but this really is a feat of endurance taken only by the very brave. Everyone has to start with a foundation course, either in the Humanities. Social Sciences, Mathematics, or Science and Technology. I tried the Humanities. Having sent off for the relevant forms, I eventually received a mass of information and was accepted. I rushed down to Blackwells, Oxford's famous bookshop, and queued with the students to pay for academic books. This gave me the importance that queuing to pay for the latest Shirley Conran certainly did not.

At 7.15 on a January morning the postman banged on the door to deliver two enormous parcels from Milton Keynes, the Open University's headquarters. Now I have seen the amount of paper for the OU A101 Foundation Course the fact that thirty acres of forest land is destroyed every minute to provide enough paper for daily world consumption makes a little more sense. Looking at my kitchen almost entirely covered with handbooks, lists, cassette tapes, units and an accumulation of other information, the thought struck me forcibly that perhaps, I should have stuck to evening classes. However, although frightened, I was determined. I attended various social evenings before the first seminar, where I met my tutor, drank wine out of a paper cup and hoped the attractive man in the corduroy suit was going to be in my group and not doing Social Sciences. (He did do Social Sciences).

At the first seminar in the Polytechnic Building our tutor, Mary Somerville, set the pace – a pace that was to continue throughout the whole course. She had tremendous energy and was always prepared to take one's pathetic attempts at intelligent answers to her questions seriously, and to help unconditionally with all aspects of the course, including me ringing her up in hysterics at 10.30 one evening because I couldn't understand at all of the meaning of witting and unwitting testimony; a requisite for my history essay. And several other crises, when, without her help, I would have given up altogether.

Every kind of student imaginable was in class. The left-wing CND ex-student graduate; the ex-nurse now housewife; the Sergeant Major from a tank regiment who had started the OU to combat the many tedious hours of inactivity in the guard room which he would have to endure whilst serving in Northern Ireland; a primary teacher; two or three secretaries; a homosexual computer operator. There was North Oxford housewife who bought her own tea in a thermos packed into a wicker basket full of notes, reference books, library books, handbooks, and digestive biscuits. She interrogated Mary intensely about statistical matters to do with the final exams or financial reimbursements or whether the unemployed amongst the class could buy cheap rail tickets to their summer school destination. Then there were several others whose lifestyle never became clear.

I looked forward to these evening seminars greatly, almost as much for the inevitable quarrels between the left-wing graduate and the Sergeant Major, as for the academic content. The LWG and soldier were the total antithesis, the one to the other. Whilst Stravinsky's music, Karl Marx's manifesto, and the paintings of Munch or Picasso, seemed totally unacceptable to one, Wordsworth, Jane Eyre and

Constable were execrable to the other. Towards the end of the seminar, when possibly attention was faltering, the two protagonists would start their battle. During the music evening, intended for serious discussion and some enlightenment for those of us who couldn't tell a violin symphony from a piano concerto (least of all understand the meaning of counterpoint) the soldier suddenly shouted out that he thought Stravinsky was a load of old rubbish and certainly not music as he knew it, if his favourite Strauss waltzes and Val Doonican were anything to go by. Chaos ensued.

To some students, the marks obtained for essays were of enormous importance; but invariably As and Bs were awarded to much the same people within each assignment. I was one of the ones for whom work did not come easily. I would spend twenty or twenty-five hours sweated writing and rewriting an essay. I had sleepless nights trying to understand utilitarianism and some of Descartes' theories and chewed through at least three biros. For all that I only had Cs, along with a few others who found the going just as rough.

Summer school at the Open University had already been thoroughly reviewed by The Sun newspaper, suggesting an orgy of incredible proportions with tutors and students leaping in and out of bedrooms, beds, bathrooms, cupboards, cars, classrooms and almost anywhere coition could possibly take place with 'lightening velocity'. My experience of summer school was of no such activities whatsoever. Studying the proposed timetable on arrival, I wondered whether there would be time for breathing, let alone 'people interaction' of any kind other than a muttered good morning on hurrying somewhere, somewhere usually so obscure, that, like White Rabbit, I was always late. When I finally arrived at the right room the blackboard was inevitably covered with unintelligible signs or words to do with music or logic or whatever, whose meaning I never entirely caught up with.

Summer schools are held throughout university vacations and last from a Saturday to a Saturday. In the first year it is a compulsory part of the course; after that it depends on the curriculum chosen. A good many students really enjoy summer school, away from home perhaps for the first time since marriage, they relish the stimulation and the opportunity to meet others with similar interests. Feeling young again and carefree, with seven days without responsibilities and with positively no washing up, is all pretty heady stuff. However, I hated it.

Bath University, where I had chosen to go for my week of enlightenment, is a serious of sprawling modern buildings, unaesthetically pleasing and about as quietly friendly and charming as Gatwick airport at an Easter break. The concrete block where my room was, although facing north, seemed to be directly in the sun's lethal rays all day, so that by early afternoon it felt like the inside of a recently used chicken hut, boiling hot, airless, sticky and humid and remaining in that state until about midnight. I wasn't in it much but if the place of refuge in alien conditions cannot 'restore the spirit and enhance the soul', your heartbeat is metaphorically weak and your condition poor. I felt strangely lonely there in spite of the 1000 or so students everywhere. There was seldom time to exchange more than a few words to anyone before rushing somewhere else, and being middle-aged and middle-class was not a bonus. The D102 Social Science Foundation Course has been widely discussed in the media for its strong leanings towards the left and Marxism. A large element of aggressive lefty students were certainly at Bath. Naturally, they could not bring themselves to accept a student so different from themselves as me. Apparently my accent or lack of it, plus age factor, betrayed me as a middle-aged, middle-class housewife dabbling in the arts. Whiling away time, they thought, and did nothing to hide their scorn. An ex-Welsh miner I met, now working at British Airways, taking the Technology Course, held particular grudges against the Conservative government and seemed to hold me partly responsible for its activities. Intense anarchical discussions at the bar in the evening if one dared to venture there at all, became tedious, and I was branded a capitalist Tory (me!) the first evening because I chose to drink gin instead of beer. Even the thought of the gin lost its appeal by the end of the week and I stayed in my room.

I did enjoy the seminars. The quality and quantity of intellectual stimulation was prodigious, particularly from the history tutor, a jolly feminist lady who smoked throughout the seminars, but who bought a new light to my understanding of primary and secondary sources and to the secrets of unravelling mysteries of ancient documents. For two packets of cigarettes she gave me an extra hour's tuition, which temporarily fed her addiction but permanently fed my mind.

I am not clear what exactly Rudyard Kipling had in mind for filling in his sixty seconds worth of distance run, but certainly in the three months after summer school and before the examination on October 25th 1982, my minutes were well filled. I started a full-time job at the beginning of September, leaving home at 8.15 and returning at 6 o'clock. After 7.05 supper (with relaxing Archers) I did OU revision for two and sometimes three hours every night. My lovely house was very neglected, dust piled up and somehow rushing to shop at Tesco on Thursday evenings I always forgot the lavatory paper. Thinking about it afterwards I assumed that subconsciously I thought I wouldn't have time to use it. Exalted though I felt in Schools − the Oxford University undergraduate examining rooms, no less − when the off was given on the examination day my hands were trembling so much I couldn't write, or even remember my identity number. I immediately dropped my packet of fruit gums onto the floor. The only thing that danced in my mind was that John Stuart Mill was born in 1806 − a fact that, having glanced at the questions would be totally useless in any answer. Sir Harold Wilson would certainly have been very proud at the amount of sheer effort, concentration, and agony that went into those three hours by the OU students. These were not the privileged university undergraduates with all day free to work, but ordinary people who at their own expense and often with very little free time, struggled on courageously in order to acquire their own sense of identity and personal achievement.

My relationship with the OU was similar to that of a lover; it produced sleeplessness, it fascinated, I thought of little else. I loved it, but I hated its power over me. It was like an on-going battle I could never escape from. I have to admit I never succeeded in putting it entirely out of my mind. It teaches self-discipline by its very solitary nature, but the seminars and self-help groups produced a sense of belonging to people all striving for a common goal. Thank God indeed, for the other students' support because no one else is remotely interested in your cut-off date or your essay and its contents. For dinner party conversations such matters rate low. Academics, or anyone who might be trying to relax at the end of the intellectual day, do not wish to discuss the Italian Renaissance or Einstein's Theory of Relativity, they are keener to argue the relative merits of Tesco or Sainsbury's if they want to discuss anything at all. The knowledge I gained by studying was entirely for myself. The pleasure now felt in an art gallery recognizing an artist not previously known, the familiarity with Beethoven's violin concerto or Chopin's preludes; or simply being able to understand some of the more obscure words in a Times leader, without the aid of a dictionary, and the pleasure that ensues, are mine alone.

In early January 1983 a letter came from Milton Keynes Examination Board. In the appropriate box was the word 'Pass'. When the exhilaration had died down there was a new decision to be made. Only five years to go now before getting the degree – was I to go on or to stop? Questions, questions. Was it worth the effort? Did I enjoy it? Would I be able to manage another year with more specialized work and less tutorial help? Could I afford it, financially or mentally? Had I enough friends and family prepared to sympathise and encourage a second year? Was it rather absurd to be a 'mature student' anyway? And so on. I found myself deliberating in a way that must be very familiar to OU students. Sifting through the pros and cons, which were about even on my list, it was passion that determined my answer. I want to know passionately. Opening the book of knowledge is like stepping into Aladdin's Cave – wonderful exciting treasures beckoning and sparkling everywhere. Obviously the Open University is not for everyone. For those who merely flirt with the idea, or quite enjoy evening classes, or who are inspired by the neighbour's boasting, or whose academic children instil a sense of competition, the trials of OU are probably too great to be undertaken. But it needs thought, working out how much time is left, how it will affect family life, and how important it really is. If it is, then it's worth at least a go. It's a challenge well worth taking. That June I signed on for another year. The battle starts again.

*   *   *

Over the last twenty years I have ben to numerous WEA classes. The Workers' Education Association is a body created, like the Open University, by the Labour Party, to provide further education for those thirsting for knowledge and who did not, by and large, find much to quench it during their school years.

Oxfordshire provided a multiplicity of these classes, and on the quest once again, I found I was studying Shakespeare in Abingdon, Philosophy in Burford, the First World War in Wantage, and English Literature almost everywhere. In my academic rush to acquire new knowledge, and the prosaic rush to drive frantically through the countryside in order to arrive at the correct college, school or where ever the classes were being held, I confused Shakespeare with Nietzsche, Nietzsche with Siegfried Sassoon, and Kafka and Kurt Vonnegut simply not read at all. (Probably because I did not care for either of them.)

I had, during my class-going years made a few assessments of the tutors' role in the classes – success or lack of it. These are they. As many more women go to classes than I do, certainly in the arts subjects (I can't vouch for Car Maintenance), male tutors are more popular than female tutors. Male tutors teaching Hardy, Byron, Wordsworth, Keats and so on are automatically associated with romantic male emotions. In these tutors can be seen, by fairly desperate and disparate women, poetic and understanding men who, given a chance, could and would quote passionate and romantic lines from favourite authors when smitten with love themselves.

In fact, these tutors would do no such thing, any more than the average Englishman whose knowledge of poetry is minimal or non-existent. But that is something these mature students would not ever wish to believe. However, to be so revered by his students is to the 'romantic' tutor's advantage. Such trust is put in his every word that he can get away with little or no class preparation. One such tutor told me that at breakfast before his morning class he opened the set book, selected a passage wherever it fell open, and talked about that passage during the two-hour session. With a coffee break and lots of questions like "Do you think Sue Brideshead really enjoyed making love to Jude or was it just another of her perversities?" which started the whole class off on personal memories of one sort or another, the tutor could then sit back and the class rolled along by itself.

Much the same power that doctors possess over patients; tutors possess over students. It is the power of superiority. They supposedly know things, important, exciting, interesting things that the rest of us would like to know but which we do not know. Their esoteric knowledge and the mystery surrounding it is their pulling power. Hence the reason passions between doctor/patient, tutor/student, teacher/pupil, vicar/choirboy or girl, abound in the hearts of the uninitiated. During the twenty years or so attending classes I have met numerous tutors, and am now of the opinion that they possess no magical qualities whatsoever. No more, at least, than could be found in any man in an average bus queue at an arbitrary bus stop anywhere.

The English Literature class I attended in Oxford was very depressing. Charles Dickens, it appeared, did not write novels that wended their way through adventures of a fairy-tale nature with an underlying social message. No, according to the new structural criticism, we were told, he simply wrote a series of words that had 'meaning' in themselves. Herman Hesse wrote in "Writing on Literature (Vol 2)" that "clever talk about art and literature has become a mockery and an end in itself, and the striving to understand them through critical analysis has done untold harm in the elementary ability to see, hear, and to be carried away." I agree absolutely with this statement.

While I was queuing to be admitted to the class in which Dickens was horribly assessed, a young punky man stood behind me drawing on his cigarette.

"What made you choose this class particularly?" I asked him. "Well, I fell out with my girlfriend last week," he said, "so I went to a film by myself, I saw *Educating Rita* and fancied Julie Walters no end. Fucking lovely she is. So, seeing this class advertised I came along hoping to meet someone here like her...".

Looking at the other students later in the evening I felt he might be disappointed. Even the youngest woman was in her thirties. I did not see him during the two classes I did attend, so assume he hadn't been lucky with a look-alike Rita, and had therefore traded in Dickens *et al* for the Duck and Drake down the road.

This literary criticism I felt, was not an exercise in which I wished to take part, so I left that class and started one of my own. It took place around my kitchen table. To find enough students I advertised in the local paper's Personal Column. (there were funny replies. I think some of the men who answered confused 'English Lessons' with 'French Lessons' as advertised in Soho shop windows in the 1950s). I also had some friends who, keen to improve their knowledge of Jane Austen, Henry James, DH Lawrence, and the like, came to the classes. An impoverished graduate, who was writing a thesis on Anthony Powell, agreed to teach us. Unlike others I have mentioned he was extremely conscientious, punctual, and spent long hours preparing our classes.

Over the two years that the classes took place, we tackled several Victorian novels and became familiar with their plots and characters. The eight members of the class (no room at the kitchen table for any more) were female, and a rare contemporary breed, happy housewives. Mutual interest in literature bound us as fluctuating prices tie other housewives, and it was a sad occasion when we had our last class. I bought several bottles of wine which we started to drink at about 10.45 am and continued drinking until lunch time. The students took turns to recite their favourite vignette, poem, or passage. Liz MacFarlane, a former member of the Royal Shakespeare Company, performed last. She read Robert Frost's poem *The Road Not Taken* which briefly is about two choices – the obvious one and the other one. The narrator took the other one. During the applause which followed her rendering there were few dry eyes, and in the following weeks I greatly missed the work and the fun of my Tuesday morning literature classes.

The mature student in adult education is a wonderful phenomenon. It brings new dimensions into life. I recommend it to everyone with any kind of thought in that direction, be it the Open University, or WEA/LEA classes or one started by enthusiasts up the street. If there is to be further unemployment, then there will be ever more unwanted free time to be filled by increasing numbers of people with little money to spend. I have a great vision for a New Britain, where people trade in their television sets and buy books instead and discover the intense pleasure they can bring. In this elixir we shall hear Chopin, Beethoven and Mozart played in the shops, music to stimulate the soul and not the terrible noise we hear in them today. (The sounds that deafen the ears and dull the senses to such an extent that after two minutes compulsory listening, I can't even think, least of all remember what I wanted to buy).

Not only book learning is important, of course, any learning in anything is important and exciting. Perhaps what I learnt was not so important. It was, simply, the learning process itself. The learning to learn, as it were. Acquiring knowledge and skills not known hitherto, not even dreamt of, producing new satisfactions in myself that I had not thought possible. I would like to think I had become wiser, and found that using wisdom through all life's vicissitudes brought me new and greater joys and contentment.

Chapter 7

Employment

It was very important that during the first few months in Oxford I should prove myself capable, and find a job. Any job. We all know that jobs are not easy to acquire even if you possess a degree, are under thirty, and have at least eight O levels and three As. With few qualifications, being over forty and out of the job market for twenty years, my chances of landing one seemed slight. But I did locate one – in a University Department. It was for one day a week, sitting in, as it were, for someone who only wanted to work four days a week. The title of this job escapes me now but the duties were as follows. I was in charge of petty cash, I had to type, answer the telephone, try to find suitable candidates willing to come in to take various tests for the department's research work; and I had to water the plants.

The people in this department were very strange, I thought. All the men looked like academic lumberjacks, resembling the cast from the film *Seven Brides for Seven Brothers*. They wore tartan shirts, jeans, or corduroy trousers, and had brown lace-up boots. They all had beards, John Lennon spectacles, and read The Guardian during the lunch hour. Left wing intellectuals, mainly, of a very familiar type in Oxford. I discovered later this breed shouts loudly about their distaste of capitalism, their dislike of conservatism, their distrust, and disdain at the way the government governs, while at the same time enjoying the very things they profess to condemn. Many of them live in large, detached houses in North Oxford, possess large cars, employ au pair girls to look after their children, and go on extensive and expensive holidays abroad in the summer, eulogizing the virtues of Marxism the while.

The only faintly exciting thing about this job was getting the payslip. I felt that I had joined the workers of the world and because of this enjoyed new confidence, and it was encouraging to know I had found a job within three months of being single. I soon saw that one day's work a week was not going to make me rich quickly. Talking to a secretary in the building who enjoyed her work and was relatively well paid, it came to me that I should try to reclaim the typing and shorthand skills I had had twenty-five years ago. So, after five months I packed in watering the plants for the lumberjacks, and set about finding a cheap typing/shorthand course.

Many courses were advertised, mainly arranged in the evenings at local schools. They all guaranteed that the student would, or could, be a tip-top secretary in a remarkably short space of time. I doubted whether I myself could learn any new skill in eight to ten weeks, dimly remembering that in my original pursuit of secretarial training it was hard work to reach the requisite speeds in nine months, to say nothing of nine weeks. Enquiring at smart secretarial schools the terms for brushing up rusty skills, I was informed that for the sum of £800 or so I could enrol for a ten-week refresher course. I settled for the College of Further Education which offered a suitable typing course for the sum of £29 for two terms, twice a week, in the afternoons. The shorthand refresher was more difficult. I had learned the original Pitman which, it seemed, was no longer taught. All varieties of new quick writing were available, but I felt I simply could not tackle them. In middle age the decline of the brain cells results in waning ability to memorize, and I was one of those who couldn't even remember much in the past when I had the full quota. So, I advertised for a private teacher who could still teach the shorthand I had learnt in the 50s. I found one who had retired to a nearby town. We negotiated, and for the next nine months I drove to her house every Wednesday morning for tuition. The morning session took an established routine whereby Mrs H. and I would discuss and view the gardens' progress since the last week, make coffee, and then retire to the dining room for dictation. Unfortunately, I have a deaf ear for vowel sounds and this in shorthand, is a complete disaster. The outline's placing on the page is indicated by the correct vowel sound and if you cannot grasp this properly a sentence which should be, for instance: 'The rut in the road' could read 'the rat in the raid'. The disasters that might ensue are obvious. However, some shorthand returned from twenty years repose and with Mrs H's encouragement and some hard work I managed to set down eighty words a minute, then decided that was probably the limit of my shorthand abilities.

In May 1982, armed with a certificate stating that I could type thirty-five words a minute without mistakes, and persuading myself I could, if pressed, manage eighty a minute in shorthand, I started searching the papers for a suitable job. My job requirements were that the post would be with quiet, pleasing people, in an historic building or similar (the sort of office that Barbara Pym's characters would work in) on a bus route. I saw one advertised in the local paper for a 'Fellows Secretary' in an Oxford College. The duties, as stated in the advertisement, sounded within the realms of my possibilities (although audio typing had not yet come my way) and I applied for it. I was asked for an interview on a Friday afternoon, just after lunch. Most Oxford Colleges are beautiful and awe-inspiring, and this one was no exception. Ever since I had read *Jude the Obscure* I felt complete empathy with him over his desire to be at Oxford University. Now, I felt, too, that being part of a college, in any capacity would be an incomparable experience.

The interview was short. (At the time I didn't know that most academics have absolutely no notion of how to converse or communicate easily with their non-academic fellow men, and that they even seem to have some difficulty with each other). I was asked why I had applied for the job and explained my Jude feelings. The Bursar explained the salary scale. My empty secretarial record for the past twenty years apparently put me on a Scale 2 basis, a salary which is somewhere comparable, I discovered, to that obtained working on the sweet counter at Woolworths. The College Secretary, a woman, was also present at the interview, and she seemed to be on my side. I did hear afterwards that she had described the said post as a job which a trained monkey could well do, and perhaps in me she saw such a one. The following day I had a letter offering me the job. I accepted, then had ever increasing anxiety about it all. My first OU exam was in October, involving hours of study, and the thought of that and learning the names of twenty-seven Fellows, and the office routine, in addition, seemed all too much. I panicked and cancelled the acceptance. But this was not to be. I was persuaded that I would manage very well (remember the monkey) and on the last day of August 1982, I started. The Fellow's Secretary's office was a large cupboard off the Principal's Secretary's office, and that is where I spent my days for the next year.

I had forgotten during my years as a housewife about office life – its trivialities, its jealousies, and its absurdities. In this college these took place in exactly the same way as they do everywhere else. Everyone, in whatever pecking order, worries about their own prestige and importance, to themselves and to everyone else. The largest worry is, it seems, that the boss/master/chief/bigwig might not appreciate the sacrifices, hard work and late hours put in by subordinates who recognize their own worth, but who are frantic that it might not be recognized by high-ups or at any rate those higher up than themselves. And it was from this particular worry that the tension in my office arose.

The College Secretary, instrumental in hiring me, had been at the College for many years. She felt herself, I'm sure, to be absolutely everything the academic staff could wish for – an agony aunt, a confidential friend, a nanny, a dining companion and primarily, of course, an efficient and reliable College Secretary. In short, indispensable. Throughout history many wars have fought and lives lost over territorial rights and in offices, if territories are not clearly defined, although lives are not actually lost, tempers frequently are.

The above College Secretary would not, or could not, delegate any interesting or responsible work. Underlings, viz me, were left therefore with copy-typing, checking lists, or filing student application forms, all which could have been done by the aforementioned monkey, as she rightly observed. She was also a woman given to dramatics. She swirled a lot, rushing hither and thither tearing at her hair and making pronouncements of a vaguely threatening nature about what she was going to say to this or that don when next encountered. When faced with him however, she never did, as far as I know, say anything of the sort.

One of my duties was to type letters from an audio machine. My previous secretarial work had not included this skill but after several attempts to coordinate the taped message with the foot pedal, and then to type correctly what the voice dictated, I mastered the art. The Fellow who dictated these letters was delightful, with a luxurious voice, pleasing to the ear. In fact, this Fellow was altogether most pleasing and I believe most of the female staff (I can't say for the one female don) were secretly in love with him. He behaved in a way that was Christian and altruistic. He was always polite, always kind and helpful wherever he could be, to anyone, regardless of where they came in the hierarchy. If I sound over-enthusiastic about this man, perhaps it is because these qualities were so apparent in him, whereas in others they were remarkably lacking.

It was difficult to resume a secretarial role again after the very different one as the lady of the manor in the intervening years. The secretary's role, I declare, is both humble, subservient and indiscriminate. A secretary can be anyone from seventeen to seventy-one. She should be able to type, take shorthand, and make the tea. She can have no previous experience or many years' experience. She can be efficient or inefficient. But basically, she is just the secretary, and when she leaves someone as good or bad will fill her place. She has as little personal identity as a forgotten wife. The optimum hope, I suppose, for a single (or married) secretary could be to marry the boss. Otherwise, having come to grips with the particular office she is in and its own routines, Shangri-La has been reached.

She is also the butt of many a smutty joke. An American man, working in an Oxford University, told me what he thought to be a hilarious story of how he came by his secretary. Sorting through hundreds of applicants applying for the job, he short-listed five. After interviewing them all he had no notion of which one to choose. They all had good references and, apparently, equally good secretarial skills. So, he enlisted the help of a male colleague. "Which one do you think I should choose?" he asked. "Well, if it were me," said his friend "I would choose the one with the biggest tits." That was the way his present secretary was given the job, which obviously proves skill and hard work doesn't always gain just rewards. Not if you are flat-chested anyway.

The job itself was dull and routine, as I suspect most jobs are where responsibility or initiative are unnecessary. But I dreaded the moments when the routine was altered, and I was summoned to take down letters in shorthand. These were dictated by dons who specialised in obscure subjects with pertinent, obscure vocabularies. As my shorthand was never strong and flowing, words like macroeconomics, renaissance, rigorous, trenchant, staunch and many others, completely flummoxed me. Returning to my office I knew that transcribing my scribbles would be much more than I could manage. Sometimes I took the shorthand home and tried to decipher it at the kitchen table. I would in desperation ring my friend Judy, who works in another college office, and ask her what she thought my outlines could possibly be. Did she, by any chance, know anything significant that had happened in Venice or Florence circa 1300? She valiantly gave me support but at the end of the evening, after hours of trying to make sense of it all, the result was usually totally incomprehensible. With this particular, precise prose, so familiar to academics and less so to the rest of us, there was absolutely no chance of substituting in my own words what I could not decipher. In my youth I worked for an advertising executive whose downfall was drink. I tumbled to the notion that if I persuaded him to dictate his letters after lunch when he had consumed large quantities of alcohol, he became both incoherent and forgetful. I was then free to type his letters as I wanted to, since he could not admit, sober the next morning, that he couldn't remember what he had dictated the day before.

The world of an Oxford College has frequently been likened to an extension of boarding school, where certainly, until recently, most of the students had spent their formative years. As I went to boarding schools myself I know the truth of this statement. It has identical debits and credits. The overriding credit must be, surely, its institutional predictability. The soothing security of knowing, for example, that unless imminent nuclear war is declared, lunch will be served at 12.45 prompt, every day, and dinner at 7.30. A College has its own life, and its own life stories. Scandal and gossip whirl about here in the same way that scandal and gossip whirl about in Ambridge, Coronation Street, Dallas, or any other community. On the debit side, I suppose, are its limitations, its total inability for flexibility. Some of the dons seemed to have little outside interests. The College is their entire world.

They were a strange lot, really, the dons. One of them was frequently to be seen in a deer stalker and cape, although the nearest grouse moor was over 500 miles away. He usually took himself off to a nearby tavern for fortification at lunch time, returning in the afternoon with a somewhat merry heart. If he was then met over the photocopying machine, pinches and hugs might be enjoyed (or might not). There was the homosexual don who darted about the covered market with a wicker basket for his shopping. There was a charming one; an attractive one fancied by many a girl student, and one who was frightened of women, although he seemed to like them, neatly balanced by one who was not frightened of women, but who didn't seem to like them. And then there was a foreigner. In order to do my work fairly a form of queuing was required.

As I worked for so many people a system of first come first served was invented, and work put in the In Tray was done in order of accession. The English race are known to be good at queuing. They stand placidly in orderly lines, not pushing aggressively as witnessed abroad. The foreign don in my college being no exception to the rougher methods of queuing employed abroad, did not care in the least about the devised system for work order, he wished his work to be done immediately. Absolutely at that moment. If I had not been in the position of secretary, which is no good position to argue from, I might, when he went into one of his rages, have told him to sod off. That very phrase I was obliged to use, finally, to a misguided don who offered me a drink of Champagne the day before I left, ostensibly to thank me for the work I had done over the year. Previously a reticent chap, I had thought, once in his room he flung his arms about me and suggested all manner of romps that he thought I might enjoy, or anyway that he might. "American secretaries enjoyed romping," he said. Disentangling myself I asked whether he flung himself upon his female students. "Certainly not," he said, "what a horrifying idea." Students are one thing, secretaries very much another, was the implication – I reacted with 'sound and fury'.

Generalizing about any group of people being one particular thing viz all West Indians are lazy, all gypsies are thieves, all Frenchmen are good in bed or whatever, is obviously ridiculous. Some secretaries are promiscuous, I daresay, but then so are some duchesses, and princesses. And some students. Others are not so. It ought to be the individual, the individual that John Stuart Mill and Thomas Carlyle so rightly and rigorously defended at the beginning of the Industrial Revolution, that should be taken into account – not who you are because of what job you do, or do not do. Most people spend their lives doing jobs, through necessity, which they do not wish to be doing. But these individuals are no less deserving of courtesy and consideration because they are less fortunate in ability or in birth, than those who had had better luck.

Before I started the job I had had a private bet with myself that I could stay in it for a year. And I did. But being a secretary wasn't quite me, my skills, it appeared did not lie in the typing direction and I admitted total defeat in shorthand. So, one year to the month later I left, and I expected the Fellows were pleased, hoping that someone more able would replace me. My overall reaction on leaving the College was one of affection. As I am hopeless at goodbyes I requested no leaving party. But the Senior Tutor who presented me with a beautiful print of the College, a bedside clock, and a £15 book token so overwhelmed me with the generosity of the Fellows I sat down in the now familiar and rather dear cupboard, and wept.

Mindless jobs are only made bearable, even enjoyable perhaps, by any fondness you may feel for your work colleagues. I was sad to say goodbye to the Principal's Secretary who had helped me on many occasions, and who had become a friend. And I was sad to say goodbye to the Principal of the College, who was, on reflection, the kindest man I had met in Oxford, or perhaps anywhere.

The conclusion I came to about jobs, is that it is not the mechanics but the dynamics that count in the end. Not so much the speeds, the skills, the technology, and the qualifications, but the human factor. The personal touch. Human complexities ever elude, and I had not even imagined I would be so affected on leaving the friends, the familiarity and security of a college world.

*　　*　　*

I found a part-time job in the autumn of that year as an Accommodation Officer in a private Tutorial College. My boss, the director, was one James Bunting. He was the antithesis of university academics, jolly, chatty, and relaxed. He actually persuaded me that I could manage more than the accommodation side of things. Totting up the accounts and working out the VAT was really very simple he said. I had had no maths tuition after the age of thirteen and the thought of my calculating, working out VAT and tackling accounts seemed outrageously funny and quite impossible. I couldn't even do my tables. Anyway, after discussions, I agreed to deal with the accommodation and, in addition and in trepidation, to pay the tutors' fees. This did involve calculation, VAT, and accounting. Once these last three mysteries had been fathomed I found 'figures were fun'.

Being the Accommodation Officer meant meeting and getting to know landladies – landladies prepared to welcome students the Tutorial College was trying to cram with knowledge which had previously eluded them. The result of poor teaching, or, more likely, truancy when they should have been working, was, for these students, failed A and O level examination papers. Thus, they needed to retake. Their parents, anxious that they should have every opportunity to go to university or 'get a good job' or at least 'get on in the world' were prepared to pay exorbitant sums to this end.

It was my job to visit and appraise the landladies and then, knowing the students, judge which one would fare best with which landlady. Virtually all the ladies I used had the same qualities. They were friendly, kind, and motherly. They enjoyed looking after the students and the students, in their turn, grew fond of them. There was much evidence of this from the many postcards placed amongst the wedding photographs, I saw on their mantelpieces, sent from all over the world. (Good for the Entente Cordiale). One favourite landlady was Vietnamese and had been a 'boat person'. She told horrifying tales of days at sea, with virtually nothing to eat and with no idea what welcome there would be when, and if, they arrived at Hong Kong. She told of the bodies of the dead, some of them her relations, who had died from illness, or just plain starvation, who were thrown overboard. After spending several months in a camp in Hong Kong, she had asked to come to England. Arriving on English shores she spoke only Vietnamese, but by the time I met her she had learnt to speak perfect English, and had married a Javanese whom she met in a restaurant he owned. So, there she was, as near as a Vietnamese could be to an English housewife, hanging up her washing in the back garden of a terraced house, a long way from Vietnam.

Another one, Mrs Adams, had no children but a quantity of large, rather fierce cats. Her house was immaculate, everything shone and sparkled. Her husband had won a variety of sports prizes which were proudly displayed everywhere – silver cups, silver shields, and silverplates. Mrs Adams was only allowed to house female students because her husband, a British Leyland worker, said he would be "ribbed by his mates at work if he left her alone with a male student", Perhaps he was right to be cautious because she was very pretty. Then there was rather a sad lady who lived on a council estate, had two small children and a large dog which she kept in the kitchen. Her problem was loneliness. She wanted a student for company much more than for the money. But I think having to contend lonely landlady, children, and the dog, whilst trying to study, was all too much. No student stayed with her for long.

Money appeared to be of less importance than other things to the landladies. They liked having a young person to care for, to cook for, and to talk to. They lived vicariously through the tempestuous lifestyles of the students. Their rewards were in being of comfort when love and passion were searing student's hearts, advising in this or that capacity, or just being the necessary listening ear at the end of the day. Indeed, my landladies were made of the proper stuff.

The students, on the other hand, were less wonderful. Most of them were lazy, stupid, and rich. They had come to Oxford to have a 'good time' and were not particularly interested in, or anxious about, their work. One affable Old Etonian, aged about 17, seemed incapable of being more than fifteen minutes without a cigarette. As smoking was banned in the College he spent quite some time puffing in the lavatory, and instead of attending tutorials he attended betting shops. It came as no surprise that at the end of four months' work (?) the result of his retake was dismal. No tears, though. His father was going to give him a job either way.

A preponderance of these students had materially everything money could buy. What many of them seemed to lack was anyone to love or care about them. These poor creatures rushed about hedonistically, in and out of different bars and different beds. They drank too much and were generally quite unable to structure their own lives now they were free from school rules or parental care. The 'poor little rich girl/boy' syndrome attracts little sympathy when compared with real deprivation, but there was something sad about them. Perhaps it was simply that they were not loved – and it showed.

The tutors whose duty it was to force facts and figures into these unresponsive minds were very different characters. They were hardworking, clever, and poor. They were always looking for work, and for food. I had to arrange various evening entertainments, to which both the students and tutors were asked. These were supposed to be drinks with a few delicacies on sticks, such as morsels of blue Brie cheese, or small chipolatas. Scant plates of nuts or savoury biscuits were also strewn about. I would set the scene for a dignified, intellectual-type evening, but my plans were always thwarted. The doors were due to open at 7 o'clock. But at three minutes to seven all the tutors were lined up outside looking like a Harrods sale queue on the first day, extremely anxious to win through. No greetings were uttered. No introductions took place. No bright light conversation drove away Jane Austen or Scott-Fitzgerald, as I had envisaged: simply, a stampede for the cheese and chipolatas. In half an hour there was absolutely nothing left

– every plate deserted, every stick on its own again. This phenomenon happened every time.

The Tutorial College employed a brilliant English tutor and Latin scholar, one John Farquhar. He was one of four children of Southern Irish parents, who had moved to Liverpool after the war, and where his father subsequently drove cranes. After winning various scholarships he went to Liverpool University and was rewarded with a First in Classics. At twenty-one he came to St. John's College to research for a D.Phil. One evening I organized an outing to Stratford, for pertinent students of English Literature and interested tutors, to see Hamlet. I drove there with John Farquhar and two students. He entranced and enlightened us with the intricacies of the many plots and sub-plots that were to unfold. He described Hamlet's agonies, his unhappiness, and his hatred for his stepmother. He talked of Ophelia and Gertrude as if he knew them personally. And Hamlet came alive. What could have been a long (four hours) evening, and if you are not familiar with certain Shakespeare plays it can be very long, was instead a delightful and enjoyable one, due to new comprehension of the play. But with real women, with flesh on their bones and blood in their veins, John was tongue-tied. In the pub, or at one of our social evenings, he rarely, if ever, spoke. I have met several brilliant scholarly people in my Oxford wanderings and, it seems, they have considerably more understanding and empathy for fictional characters, than they have for their fellow men.

Trilby, a lively feminist white Jamaican, was the PA and secretary. I had thought myself quite worldly wise until I met

Trilby, but this obviously was not so. Her use of four-letter words was proficient, particularly during the graphic descriptions of her multifarious sex life. She delivered speeches on anti-apartheid matters at the Co-op on Wednesday evenings, or organised marches through Oxford on Saturday mornings. But she was amusing, an appealing Peter Pan. James, Trilby, and I got on so well. It was the first place in Oxford, I knew, where laughter was *de rigeur.* After the students had gone home and there was nobody about, James, an actor manque, and excellent at the Yorkshire accent, did some quality imitations of Les Dawson doing the Northern Mill Girls or Peter Cook with his 'miles of boring space' sketch. But perhaps to be successful at business you have to be less carefree than we were, because at the end of the year the College closed. Tutorial Colleges had mushroomed up all over Oxford, competition for students was fierce and the shoestring budget broke. James went out of business and Trilby, and I were out of jobs.

I had, nonetheless, proved to myself, in this job, that I was capable of hitherto unknown abilities. I had conquered the calculator, and now understood Value Added Tax, and some easy accounting. For someone who had thought two years previously that counting the change in my purse was a fairly arduous task, I felt suitably proud of myself.

So many of us do not know of what we are capable, since we are seldom put to the test. When, through necessity or courage or whatever, we try something new and seemingly impossible, it comes as a lovely surprise that, on the contrary, it is not only possible, but exhilarating, rewarding, and fulfilling. In this job as Accommodation Officer I found it to be so.

*   *   *

Staying in a country hotel over a November weekend in the Cotswolds, I was suddenly inspired to be a hotel receptionist. In this particular hotel a roaring log fire burnt in the grate, and the whole reception area seemed welcoming and cosy. An ancient black telephone sat on the desk, presumably to take the bookings, and a large bound book for arrival signatures. That seemed to be all. The receptionist was busily reading a book and I realized I envied her job.

On returning to Oxford, aglow with enthusiasm, I scoured the papers for a similar occupation for myself. I rang the Job Centre, where incidentally they had a vacancy for a still-room maid in a smart hotel in Woodstock, which they were finding difficulty in filling. The job was from 6pm until midnight, six nights a week at a rate of £1.20 per hour with one tea break – the sort of conditions that makes unemployment seem desirable. I then telephoned possible hotels in the town and in the peripheral countryside (remembering the Cotswold hotel) – but had no luck. A few weeks later I heard of a vacancy going in an Oxford hotel and rang immediately. I spoke to the proprietor who asked me to start evening work the following night.

The first disappointment on arrival was a glance at the reception area. It was set up in a sort of cupboard. This was

74

practically filled with a large grey menacing telephone machine which incessantly winked and blinked red and green lights indicating constant use from callers and guests. The desk I had envisaged was simply a ledge, and no bound visitors' book either. The hotel owner, a middle-aged jolly woman, introduced herself, eyed me up and down, and then announced that I was not to be the receptionist, but hotel cook. My heart turned cold: me, the cook? Cooking has never been my *forte*. I have been known to dissolve into hysterics at the thought of six to dinner, with all day to arrange it. While all this was running through my mind we descended into the basement. Entering a small room I saw a large variety of brown nylon overalls (with white collars) in heaps all over the floor. Find one to fit, the woman said, then come up to the kitchen quickly because guests start asking for dinner after 6.30. it was then 6.05. I was overwhelmed with that strange feeling, now frequently experienced, of total unreality. What on earth was I doing here, sorting out a suitable brown nylon uniform to wear in the position of cook in a 2-star hotel in the City of Oxford where I had come to seek academic excellence?

For some reason I had decided to bring a wig with me. Perhaps I thought that, should I have had the occasion to venture into the hotel kitchen, the smell of burning chip fat, absorbed into my hair, would be very nasty for days to come. I struggled into a uniform that smelt strongly of tobacco, donned the wig, and with beating heart went to find the kitchen. There, I stammered to the proprietor that I wasn't much of a cook. Not to worry, she said, that was of no importance. If I could read, boil water, and switch on a microwave oven, then I had all the requirements necessary. She then showed me a large deep-freeze in which all the food was kept. Duck à l 'Orange, Mixed Grill, Pheasant, Chicken Mornay. All choices, all there, everything a gourmet could want, frozen into unrecognizable cold flat slabs, sealed in plastic bags. The system of cooking was as follows. Boil a large pan of water and leave it on the stove, boiling. Similarly, fill two large saucepans with cooking fat, boil and leave boiling. Switch on the microwave oven. The guests came in swiftly at 6.35pm. I wondered if they were regulars who knew what to expect.

If the request was Duck à l 'Orange (or anything else) I ran to the deep freeze, selected the correct frozen packet, threw it into the boiling water, the frozen chips into the boiling oil, and yesterday's vegetables into the microwave oven to heat up. That was the simple dish. The more complicated mixed grill, for instance, needed a little more dexterity. Before putting some of it into the boiling water, I had to extract the sausages and chops to immerse them into the second saucepan of boiling fat. The next two hours of the evening are a sort of haze in the memory, in more ways than one. The heat in the kitchen was probably about 90°, the atmosphere hot, dank and misty, making it difficult to breathe. My mind was in neutral. Actually, a certain intelligence is needed to remember how long each of these revolting creations had been boiling, sizzling, and reheating. I suppose it must have been about 9 o'clock when the rush stopped and the commercial travellers slipped out of the hotel, hoping, no doubt, for a victorious evening where the bright lights beckoned. The washing up then had to be done, mostly by hand. At 10.15 I was told I was now to assume bar duties. The bar itself looked like a scene from a B-movie where the gangsters meet to discuss the Final Plan, masses of red lights, and overflowing tin ashtrays. The smell of stale tobacco and beer was suffocating. I remember thinking: I can't leave now, this nightmare has to end at 11 o'clock, so I agreed to become the barmaid.

The only customers were two fairly drunken Turks, who indicated with much arm waving and flashing of gold teeth that they wished their glasses to be replenished. Two Kirmizi Saraps, they said. I stared in horror at the hundreds of different bottles containing all sorts of incredible alcoholic beverages, and wondered which could possibly contain Kirmizi Sarap. Somehow, by pointing and gesticulating, I managed to organize the drinks. But then came a new worry: How did I open the till? It was locked, and I had no key. By this time I was feeling a little like I imagined Alice did when the car kept appearing and disappearing – slightly mad, a little hysterical. A mirror at the end of the bar revealed my appearance, the wig askew, nylon overall sticking darkly to me, sweat pouring down my face. A humorous thought struck me. In contrast to my evening in the sleazy bar off the Woodstock Road, that very night my sister was dining at Kensington Palace with Princess Margaret. I thought God's purpose for us, individually, was not so easy to follow at that moment. Before I left at 11.00 pm I had to return to the kitchen for one more duty: the floor had to be washed. Finally, exhausted, and smelling strongly of chip fat, I was allowed home. I had earned £8.

*   *   *

I did try for several other jobs, without success. I went for an interview at the local newspaper. They were looking for a telesales-person. The man who interviewed me was the stereotype of a newspaper man as portrayed in all television series. He had no charm whatsoever, talked very quickly out of the side of his mouth, and chain smoked. His telephone rang every two minutes and to each caller he spoke briefly and brusquely.   An imitation of Humphrey Bogart perhaps.

"As a matter of fact," he said, when he had asked my age "we do like younger female staff".

"Why?" I enquired innocently, "are they better at telesales in some way?"

"Oh God no" he said, "they aren't better at telesales; but of course they are better to look at, so that keeps the male staff happy and then they are better at the telesales." Ah well….

Looking back, I wonder whether my anxiety to find a job was to prove something to myself, or for the money, or the experience or what? The answer was probably a culmination of many things. The longed-for and looked-for separate identity women so much wish they had, and believe is not to be found in being a housewife, but can be found in a job. Any job. With a job comes a wage and that produces some independence. A certain pride is felt in being chosen for a job and a certain satisfaction in executing your duties.

The main reason that people go to work is for the money. Nothing more. If they had a choice, it appears, they would not work where they do work; in fact, they wouldn't work at all. For people in the strong position of having a job it is easy to envisage the delights of endless free time. This idea is, of course, rubbish, as hours of time stretching away into the distance without any particular way of filling them is both frightening and depressing. I think people do need rules, structure, and discipline for a contented life and a job, by its nature, determines these. Working again after twenty fallow years was exciting. The jobs were irrelevant. But acquiring them was the first step to restoring confidence and achieving independence – two major goals in my single life.

Chapter 8

Practicalities and Economics

I was completely ignorant when I came to Oxford about most practicalities. Once single, this became clear almost immediately. This chapter, is not, dear reader, one to be skipped for its lack of excitement if you are bent on that, or have just become newly single. I wasted much money and energy through my own stupidity, lack of expertise and general gullibility. So please take heed.

The unimaginable horror of maintaining a car

I had arrived in Oxford driving a one-year-old Renault 30, in near perfect condition. But it was much too expensive to run, and I decided to sell it. I went alone to Luxicars, a garage dealing specifically with Renault, to 'do a deal'. The slick salesman I dealt with convinced me that Renault 30s were really obsolete. They might, with luck, sell for scrap, he said, but certainly no private buyer would want one. There was absolutely no demand for them whatsoever, he assured me with a wave of his smooth hand. "Who after all, would want a large expensive-to-run vehicle in this day and age?" he asked. Now it would be a different matter completely, he explained if I was selling a small vehicle such as a Renault 5, which incidentally, was a model he would recommend. And, coincidentally, he had just such a one. A Renault 5, twelve years old, but only owned by one lady driver, who hardly ever used it but kept it in a cosy garage. Imagine that; one lady driver, perfect condition and hardly ever used! What a bargain. And in 1982 unbelievably, I actually believed him. So, a transaction took place. I paid £1,400 for a twelve-year-old Renault 5, with 56,000 miles on the clock and Luxicars credited me £600 in part exchange for my Renault 30, just one year on the clock. It was all perfectly legitimate. No one forced me to sell low and buy high. Indeed, I thought I had quite a good bargain. I had bought a small, desirable inexpensive to run, Renault 5, and Luxicars, in part exchange, had acquired an apparently undesirable and seemingly unsellable Renault 30. The salesman must have gone out at lunchtime and drunk Champagne to his success at felling another pathetic and inexperienced woman. The thought still makes me sick.

I left the garage in my innocence, quite happy. My friend Michael, usually so supportive and encouraging when told of my various activities, went completely white, shook a bit, and seemed unable to speak when I told him of my bargain. To have been so duped by a car salesman's line of rubbish and untruths was, to him, incredulous. (My brother-in-law and the vicar held the same view). I tried unsuccessfully therefore to stop my cheque, recover the Renault 30 and return the Renault 5. But I was too late, the cheque had been cashed. The bargain had truly been struck and I was the loser. Two weeks later I saw the Renault 30 parked outside a large house in North Oxford. The house did not, at a glance, look like a scrapyard. The worst punishment for my folly was that I felt such a fool and was constantly reminded of my stupidity by my friends and loved ones.

Car stories are very dreary so I will keep the facts to the minimum. I will simply say that for three years the Renault 5, when on the road could not be faulted. However, it wasn't often on the road. It had one major deficiency. It wouldn't start. Apparently, it did not like any weather condition. It felt no joy in the warmth of the sun, nor in the winter cold, nor in the wind or in the rain, and sulkily refused to budge. Several garages tried to cure this problem, but it was totally unresponsive to all efforts. Three years later, when my aunt died and left me a small legacy, I decided that a new car was top priority.

This time, I thought, no charlatan or rogue in a garage is going to outwit me. I shall approach buying a car in a thoroughly wise way – much as an Army officer might plan an attack, with rigour and efficiency. I sent for a copy of Which Magazine's special issue dealing solely with cars. It described in great detail the different makes, their good points and their drawbacks. For instance, small roomy ones with hatchbacks, large roomy ones economical in petrol with a place for the dog, sports cars for Yuppies, or stout and reliable ones for the older couple. In fact, a large variety of combinations each of which had professional recommendations.

After weeks of deliberation, I decided that the right car for me was the Vauxhall Astra GL 1300. It suited all my requirements and was thoroughly recommended as a smallish comfortable car, inexpensive on petrol but full of life. Having made that decision I now had to find and buy a second-hand model. I bought several copies of the Thames Trader (a magazine advertising used cars in the area) over the ensuing weeks, marking suitable contenders. But finding and buying the perfect car is not easy. Often ones that sounded suitable had already gone by the time I rang, or the advertisement had neglected to say that although the car was in 'perfect condition' and only two years old, it has somehow travelled some 55,000 miles. It is true, apparently, that after 100,000 miles a car engine is in its dotage, and the rest of the pieces and parts are none too sprightly either. In fact, they all need replacing – including the engine. Anyway, becoming by now a little desperate (the Renault's insurance had run out) I saw one advertised as being in perfect condition, three years old, and only £2,500 because the owner was going abroad. I made an appointment to see it the following evening in Newbury. The house was in Newbury's affluent suburbs and the lady selling it was a middle-aged, middle-class Telegraph reader who organized her local PTA. Dependable, I thought. She and her husband were 'devoted Christians' and were selling this car for friends, a couple who had had to rush off to Canada to spread the word. Having bought this car, reputed to be in good condition and finding this not to be so, I concluded the mote in their own eye should have been examined before they rushed abroad to set others to rights about theirs.

I knew that it was common practice to call the AA or some expert to check any car before buying, but several people had seen the car that day and there were more to come. The woman was anxious to sell it (not surprisingly) and as the AA takes approximately four days before going out to look at a potential car, I had to buy it immediately or lose it. It looked in excellent condition and during a ten minute 'drive around' it seemed perfect. I bought it.

Two days later I drove it back to Oxford. During this short journey I discovered that driving over fifty miles per hour the steering wheel wobbled so much that I couldn't hold on to it, the heating didn't work, and the light switch came away from the dashboard when I tried turning the lights on. And that was only the beginning. I feel it is important to note this 'perfect' car's deficiencies, so that potential trusting females might benefit from mistakes. These are the completely new parts I have had replaced or repaired in the last fourteen months:

3 tyres	1 light switch	1 car engine
1 choke	1 starter motor	1 gasket
plugs	1 battery	1 alternator
1 set of keys	1 ignition switch	1 exhaust pipe
1 front offside	1 offside	back-brake
shock absorber	suspension leg	shoes
1 fuel pipe from	points	
pump to		
carburettor		

In addition, I had the fan belt tightened, the steering wheel adjusted, and the tyres balanced. The bill for these 'adjustments' has so far come to £1,063.25.

Anger, agony, disbelief, fear, and frustration are just a few emotions I have undergone over the months worrying about this car, to say little of having to find the money to pay for it.

Garages are still a male bastion, and my conclusion is that a woman should never go to them alone unless she has done a car maintenance course and is assertive by nature. A man is imperative in car transactions and single women should bribe, borrow, or pay one to accompany her when car dealing, either buying or just organizing repairs.

I have just learnt to ask the right questions about dirty points and plugs, and/or checking the carburettor and I do now know that the electrical parts are nothing whatsoever to do with the engine – but still. I have learnt too late. Cars and their curious temperamental ways are really beyond me and are, also, of little interest. I simply wish one thing of my car, that it should be reliable. So far this wish has not been granted and sometimes I seriously think that I would be married again if I could find a man to take charge of the dreaded car with all its whims and fancies, and bills. The last time I took the beastly thing to the garage the mechanic, now very familiar with the perfect Astra, declared desperately that either my car had a jinx on it, or it was what is known, in the trade, as a 'Friday night' car. This is the one, apparently, that is the last on the line to be assembled on Friday night before the weekend break when everything is put together in great haste but without much care. I strongly suspect my Astra was one of these, since short of replacing the windows and doors there is not much left of the original model. And not a great deal left of my savings. CAVEAT

EMPTOR, Let the buyer beware, is a quote I shall never forget when buying anything. I strongly endorse its truth.

The ghastliness of gas bills and budgeting

I had had gas fired central heating fitted in the house when I bought it. The plumber who installed it conscientiously explained to me how the clock, instrumental in working the thermostat, should be set to regulate the hours and temperature needed during any twenty-four hours. His explanation seemed a little complicated, but I was too proud to go over it all again. The result was that at the end of the first cold water quarter I had a gas bill for £489.93. It was terrible and frightening. Fortunately, my mother, always generous, agreed to lend me the money to pay the bill. But even she, biased, was incredulous that I didn't understand the workings of my own boiler. I abandoned pride and asked the plumber back. He came, was very understanding, and soon its intricacies became clear.

I rang the Gas Board and spoke to a charming woman, one Mrs Hall. I asked her the best way to pay the gas bill on a limited income and she suggested she should send me a Gas Budget plan. On receiving it I worked out how much gas I used weekly, on average through the year. With this knowledge the gas bill in now paid through a Banker's Order, so much every month throughout the year. Consequently, I am spared the agony of the dreaded brown envelope on the mat waiting to frighten me when I come down in the morning, demanding large sums of money from the Gas

Board. If you want to learn to love your boiler, I recommend this system.

The subtle approach to an interesting wardrobe

Buying new clothes is good for the morale and bad for the bank balance. With not much money to spare and clothes a luxury, not a necessity, Harrods, and Laura Ashley are simply places to window shop, not actually to buy. Nor, indeed, is anywhere else. So, wondering how I could have something different, I discovered the joys of shopping at Oxfam and other second-hand shops. From Oxfam I once bought two corduroy jackets, one denim waistcoat and a pair of leather boots, hardly worn, all for £27. I had them cleaned and no one could tell that they didn't come from Harrods. Perhaps they originally did, since many rich women, to make themselves feel better about being rich, I suppose, gather last year's fashions from their wardrobes in the spring and magnanimously take them to charity shops. (passing through the eye of a needle is not going to be easy, after all, and men and women of all means need all the help they can get). Depending on the area some shops have much better things than others so it is worth going to several areas.

I sorted through my own clothes and divided them into three heaps. To keep and alter, to sell, or sadly to put into the dustbin. Some I kept were really very old, circa 1960s, but still great favourites. I become very fond of my clothes. I find it as heart-breaking as saying goodbye to an old friend when I finally discard a tattered cardigan. I'm a great recycler; I cut up some of the old dresses and made them into skirts, and some of my long skirts I altered to three quarter length. I needed the familiarity of my old clothes while so many other things in my world were changing. As in Heathcliff's and Cathy's alliance, I feel that my clothes are me and I am them.

I discovered, too, the wonders of the car boot sales. These weekend diversions have crept over here from America and are in excellent invention. In my house there is no storage space. All the clothes I was less fond of, but which still had life left in them, I took to sell at car boot sales. The local paper tells you where these took place: it is usually on a Saturday or Sunday in the local school or college car park. By paying £4 or £5 at the entrance, you park your car and display, as attractively as possible, the contents of your boot.

I have had many an adventure in the pursuit of people to buy my old clothes. At a car boot sale combined with a fete in a farm field outside a twee black-and-white Tudor-cottagey village I met and talked to many disparate people. I spoke to a gypsy woman who wove spells. She was 59 but looked 30. (If her youthful appearance was due to her magic and she had had any business sense, she could have been rich). Her daughter, she told me, had married the son of the Squire. I saw the Squire, red-faced, fat, and jovial, shouting enthusiastically to the home team during a tug-of-war against a neighbouring village. (I wondered, watching him, what he did with a gypsy girl in his bed. He didn't look blessed (?) with sensuality, but you can never tell.

A chatty lady from the local garage took a great fancy to four pretty velvet pinafore dresses I had for sale. I was selling them because, sadly, in my middle age I had outgrown them: they were too small and too young. She rushed off to try them on in the makeshift outside lavatory. It was built out of straw bales, put up outside the cowshed. Her return was triumphant. They fitted her and she bought all four. I was triumphant too. I made £24. A retired accountant, who was also the church warden, was trying to sell some rather tired looking plants from the boot of his car, next to me. Giving up early, he asked me to choose something from my boot, for his wife. Her size, he thought was something like mine, but then again, he couldn't really remember. He had probably been married for fifty years and between breakfast and lunch he had forgotten her shape. I selected two items that I was selling for my sister. Her clothes are definitely superior to mine, so I charged £10 for a tweed skirt, and £8 for a jacket of Italian origin. He was delighted with them, and I made over £70 that day.

The less choice I have in choosing anything, the better. So much time and energy, which I do not wish to waste, goes into choice. My aim was to establish a uniform for summer and winter, in order to eliminate the worry and bother of what to wear every day. This plan has been very satisfactory and I now have three skirts for winter, all the same style, and two pinafore dresses. I wear the winter clothes for nine months of the year and should it be warm in the summer I have an identical wardrobe, in cotton, for this eventuality.

In the same way that I reduced food choices and found things much easier, reducing clothes choices has been a great relief and getting dressed in the morning is now no trouble at all.

How to take the torment out of the rates

Rates do not go away by putting the bill in the kitchen drawer, neither do they contract. Rates simply go up and, like death, are inevitable. To minimize the agony of paying them I find monthly instalments are preferable to finding a lump sum each April. The Council is quite agreeable to payment this way.

The charm of investing in a Building Society: how not to be swindled of your savings

If you do happen to have a Fairy Godmother who leaves you some money there is no better place to put it, I think, than in a building society. Money matters seem unbelievably complicated to the uninitiated, and unscrupulous people can relieve you of your savings with no great conscience. Furthermore, they leave you with no redress. There are lots of building societies to choose from – The Bristol and West being my choice. It seems to be smaller and cosier than the better-known ones and a sense of family intimacy pervades the office I go to. The staff are extremely helpful and friendly, always prepared to explain anything I need to know and which I do not understand – like percentages and things of a similar mysterious nature. I have consequently grasped the fact that I can achieve a higher rate of interest for my investments at a Building Society than I can at the Bank. Building Societies, I know, do not conjure up excitement, but then they are not meant to. Safety is the adjective that suits them and me. I like to believe that, like a nanny, they will look after me and my best interests, (I'm sure Rupert Brooke would have gone to one). They are a sort of caring aunt. And this is just what one wishes to embrace being in the single position, something secure and solid with no risks attached.

The importance of not letting the dreaded function of shopping and cooking haunt you

Terence Rattigan's play *Separate Tables* is thought-provoking. But the thought that provokes me most is not that a spiritless woman, aroused by passion, overcame her fear, and braved the enemy, but, how lucky all those people were, living in a hotel. They had absolutely no worries whatsoever about what they were going to eat; either about shopping for it or puzzling about the menu. They just sat down and ate it. There are many disparaging things said about institutional type food, especially English food. It is usually boiled cabbage and shepherd's pie followed by sago pudding, or perhaps in more modern places, instant curry followed by instant whip. But if I do not have to think about any of its journey, from mind to table as it were, anything is delicious. 'Life is so every day' someone complained once. Food is certainly every day and I think things would have been better arranged if we had had six days in which to labour and eat, and on the seventh everything, including eating, stopped. This would have been a proper day of rest, at least for the one in the family who shops and cooks. Eating on my own I find is quite a different event from family repasts or communal meals. The thought of making something tempting for myself, on an everyday basis, has no appeal at all. During lunch I listen to the news and at supper I listen to the Archers. The food I eat is of secondary importance. But, with the increasing waistline rapidly acquired by not eating the right things – I decided to make a little more effort in shopping and preparation. Otherwise, I saw myself as the Fat Lady at the Fair. Practising food economy creates practising vegetarians, since buying meat is a luxury, not often considered. But I do buy kippers and haddock since fish is a must, apparently, whereas meat is not. Marks and Spencer, Waitrose and Sainsbury's all produce tempting packaged pies, fish pies, meat pies, chicken pies, vegetable pies and an assortment of frozen pies. The pies are made of good things and are easy to cook since no culinary expertise is necessary – only the ability to open the oven – and delightful to eat. Naturally, there's a snag. The price. They are expensive and add pounds to the food bill. I have one or two stored in the freezer in case of an unexpected guest for a candlelit dinner or whatever, but otherwise I do not buy them. It is quite easy, quick, and cheap to make stews and soups out of fresh vegetables. Yoghurts are good for pudding and fresh fruit is a taste that I have acquired, even for unamusing apples. (Perhaps the thought that they are so good for me makes the difference). I spend about £20 a week on food. My basic shopping list is fresh vegetables and fruit, cereals, wholemeal bread, Flora, fish and sometimes a chicken.

Chapter 9

Miscellaneous Adventures

The singles club

In 1957 I 'came out', I was a debutante. This procedure, for the uninitiated, was when at the age of 17 or 18 curtseying to the Queen at Buckingham Palace, whirling about at balls, attending Ascot Races and Henley Regatta, plus rushing up to Scotland in September for more balls and races, established the fact that you were grown-up and marriageable. Ready for marriage, that is, with an eligible ex-public schoolboy. Men in the Brigade of Guards, or at Sandhurst perhaps, merchant bankers, stockbrokers, barristers, solicitors, and men with titles were sought after and fought over, by zealous mothers anxious to see their daughters 'settle down' with the 'right' sort of man.

For me, being a debutante was a failure. Undeniably I had two serious disadvantages. I was short-sighted and dumpy. The choice of spectacle frames in the 1980s is not as plentiful as one would wish, but in the 1950s there was virtually no choice at all. I had a pair shaped like blue plastic butterflies in Dame Edna Everidge style. If I wore them at dances in order to see, no one asked me to dance, and if I didn't wear them, I could see nothing. Strapless dresses were in fashion, which on tall thin girls looked marvellous but which did not suit me in the least. However, despite protests my mother, determined that I should be properly launched, bundled me off to The Ritz, The Savoy, Claridges and The Dorchester where I danced with, or at least mingled with dukes, earls, lords, varying degrees of aristocrats, and the odd foreign prince. But from the debris one good thing did emerge. I discovered dancing is a lovely way of taking exercise, without getting tired or bored, as I do with almost all other exercise. This feeling for dancing has never left me and I frequently dance alone in my kitchen with Flute, the cat, as my audience. But Andy, a single girlfriend, wished me to accompany her to a club she knew. She enthused about the music and dancing, the fun and excitement to be had at the Singles Club dancing evenings held on Thursdays, at a hotel in Wheatley, just outside Oxford. They were only £1.75, she said tickets (in 1982), and well worth the money. I was quite easy to persuade since I thought having a partner after several years without one would be quite a novelty.

What to wear was a dilemma as my wardrobe did not run to suitable dresses or skirts to dance in. (In public). After trying on various garments with a view to attracting partners I settled for a black cotton skirt, an old, flowered silk shirt, and lots of my daughter Jessica's jewellery — bright pink earrings and necklace. I picked Andy up just after nine and as we approached the hotel, I felt very nervous. We both admitted afterwards that had the other one said that it was all a mistake and that the wish to go dancing had quite vanished, great relief would have been felt, and we would have gone home. But we admitted no such thing. The hotel car park was almost full when we arrived, and we joined a furtive and hurrying crowd heading towards the entrance. Here was a slight hold-up. It was the queue to pay for the tickets and then, in addition, to be scrutinized by the management to see that our clothes were smart enough to pass for evening wear. (Men had to wear ties). You also had to declare that you were single and over 25. We went to hang our coats up in the Ladies, where there was a general air of excitement. Masses of new make-up were applied – more lipstick to already lustrous red lips, to eyes more blue, and to lashes more mascara. Calvin Klein would have recognized his monstrous regiment of women. They were all there, in every guise. All sizes, ages, heights and degrees of sexual attractiveness. But there was one common denominator – everyone was single. I suspect, although I have no evidence, that the aims were also similar: to have a good night out and possibly find 'Mr Right'.

Andy and I decided to start our evening in the bar. Remembering the old joke about "two gin and tonics and I'm anybody's", I thought at least if I had one, my knees and hands would stop shaking. The band was playing very jolly, catchy, tunes from the fifties era onwards. I felt a touch of nostalgia hearing songs from big musicals like Oklahoma, Paint your Wagon, Annie Get Your Gun, Showboat and so on. Disco lights of different colours winked over the dance floor. But in the bar, there were only small table lights, with red lamp shades, discreetly dotted about. I wondered whether the darkness in the bar, where friendships were struck up, was a subtle plan on behalf of the management. It was difficult to tell in the gloom the features of the person you were talking to, and this, in most cases, was a definite advantage. By the time you reached the dance floor and saw your partner's face under the light, or he saw yours, it was too late to change your mind about a dance.

My first partner, Les, was an ex-policeman. He hinted at being in possession of numerous MI5 type secrets which he might reveal, he said, should we later become more intimate. But he was hopeless at dancing, so I left him. Unlike debutante dances where, if I was abandoned I spent the rest of the evening in the Ladies, at the Singles Club after the end of a dance, partners thanked each other and returned to their original table. At Australian parties, apparently, all the men stick together at one end of the room while the women huddle together at the other. At the singles club I observed a definitely Australian influence. Men of all descriptions stood still and silent, grasping drinks. The only thing that moved was their eyes, which slunk around, seeking a woman to their taste.

I must have had some of the right qualifications since I was asked to dance, in quick succession, by a motor mechanic, a draughtsman, and a milkman. Then I met Terry, an RAF engineer from Brize Norton. He was about 25, and wore a smart blue suit and a forces tie. He had a short back-and-sides haircut. His appearance was ordinary and his conversation non-existent, (except about divorce or separation, a topic of conversation where everyone had a story), but he was a really amazing dancer. We jived, rock-and-rolled, tangoed, waltzed, Charlestoned, and twisted for two hours, and I loved it. Unfortunately, Terry had the same constraints on him as Cinderella – midnight was his deadline for leaving. He had to return to base.

I danced a last dance with an electrician, one Pete, who was wearing a blue nylon shirt, green tie, and beige terylene trousers. With the later hour the music had become romantic. A rendering of favourite Des O'Connor, Val Doonican, and Julio Iglesias' love songs were sung by the enthusiastic band leader, doing his best. It wasn't bad and there was a feeling of something in the air. 'By the time I get to Phoenix' was playing when Pete cleared his throat to speak. We were dancing quite close and my fingers were stuck to his nylon shirt. Perhaps it will be something romantic, I thought, but in fact what he said was: "Looking round this room, I'm most disappointed. I would definitely say that the club I go to in Maidenhead contains a much higher class of person. Do you know what I mean....?"

The approach to women at dances by dukes, earls, lords, electricians, mechanics or what-you-will is indubitably much the same, it seems. If you are chosen to dance, it is with the idea that, after a bit of bald flattery, a few sexy dances with the electric current low, and a run-down on their astounding abilities in bed, you will rush home with them to see the evidence, and test its truth. As for me, the only difference between men at dances, wherever they are, is whether they can dance or whether they cannot. And as I found a better partner at the Singles Club, Wheatley, than I ever did at The Savoy, London, for my £1.75 that is where I would rather go for a good dancing night out.

Rape Crisis Centre

Mandell Creighton, a nineteenth century ecclesiastic, said: "No people do so much harm as those who go about doing good." Now, twenty-five years after I started on the doing-good road, I would agree with him. It would be a rash generalization, and wrong to suggest that all do-gooders were harmful, but certainly the motives for wanting to do good are often questionable, and the results often undesirable. If it is true, and it seems to be, that altruism doesn't exist, the only reason that people are 'wonderfully self-sacrificing' or whatever, is because that is what they wish to be. Naturally this does not apply to anyone looking after a disabled member of the family, or some such, who therefore, has no choice.

Most of the women and men I met at various voluntary activities were over thirty-five, with time to spare, looking for something to fill their empty lives. In my married life, I was one such a woman.

Many voluntary organizations encourage their volunteers to see themselves as 'counsellors'. (This terrible word means nothing superior whatsoever, but is simply someone who listens, or talks, or who gives good or bad advice). The 'counsellor' then acquires a sense of power which otherwise she or he would not possess. There are indeed training schemes to train volunteers from being 'ordinary folk' into 'caring counsellors'. How to acquire a 'caring' voice is also taught so that whatever filth is metered out to you on the telephone, at one of those establishments, you have to keep repeating "I know how you feel," in a caring voice – even if you haven't the least idea what it must be like to be masturbating in a telephone box.

Knowing that there are others sadder and more bereft than oneself can have a cheering effect on the listener. When I was unhappy years ago, I had many so-called friends. I have many less now, and the reason, I think, is that my present contentment is a touch dull, whereas my misery, for them, was exalting. One of the characters from Aldous Huxley's *Ends and Means* said: "I can sympathize with people's pain but not with their pleasure. There is something curiously boring about someone else's happiness."

Not entirely cured of my somewhat manic desire to be of help to the community, I answered an appeal I heard on Radio 4. It was for people to man the telephones at the local Rape Crisis Centres. They were apparently short of volunteers to perform this activity. I rang locally, and spoke to a woman who told me to come to a meeting taking place on the following Wednesday evening, at 7.30. The address was in the Cowley Road, which, although I have grown fond of it, is not a place to be when the light has faded. Cowley has been described as dirty, lawless, dangerous, and noisy. This is an accurate description.

When I arrived at the given address, from outside I could see one light. It was coming from an attic room. I pushed the front door open and found myself in a dark, gloomy hall. Following the light I started up dirty, bare, rickety stairs, until I reached the top landing. I knocked on the door and was asked in. In this bizarre room the floor space was almost entirely covered with old mattresses. On one of them sat a young woman, but, to my conventional and untrained eye, she could have been a man. She wore a man's shirt, red braces, trousers, and bovver boots. A donkey jacket was by her side, with a tin of roll- your-own navy cut tobacco sticking out of the pocket. "Hello" she said, "I'm Linda – I'm on duty for Lesbian Line.". "Oh" I said, confused, "but I thought this was the meeting place for the Rape Crisis Volunteers." "It is," she said, "they take place in the same room – this room. Why don't you sit down?" Since there were no chairs, I sat down on a mattress and looked about me.

The walls were entirely covered with posters unflattering to me. viz: All men are rapists – Penis Power is woman's violation – Rape in Marriage is a crime, and many more of a similar nature.

There were pamphlets and printed sheets littered about, all pertaining to feminist causes and female rights. Soon women started arriving. They were between twenty and twenty-five, and mainly Linda-look-alikes, although there was one in an Indian skirt. A fierce-looking androgynous person asked me who I was and why I was there. I muttered about the radio appeal which seemed to satisfy her and the meeting began. The room was very small and with nine people in it, mostly smoking roll-ups, the atmosphere quickly became pungent. I was squashed between two women in donkey jackets who smelt quite strongly of sweat, tobacco and beer. Fervently I wished that I had not answered this particular call for help, and that I could run back home. But that was not possible without drawing attention to myself so reluctantly I stayed.

Among several points to be brought up on the agenda, the boycotting of *Miss Oxford* remains the most prominent in my mind. It was to decide what role each one would play in seeing that this event did not take place. Or, if it did, it would only do so with maximum harassment. Various tactics were discussed, including bottle throwing, tyre slashing, crowd agitation and several other destructive ideas. Suddenly I was asked what I was going to do in the way of disruption. My heart beat faster as I suspected that, in this particular company, mentioning that I was a magistrate and therefore, ineligible to fight the battle, was not appropriate or appreciated. Indeed, there could have been positive hostility. The quiet and gentle heroines of Mrs Gaskell and Jane Austin that I so revere were about as far removed from these women as could possibly be. I declined with some excuse. At 10.30pm the meeting adjourned and everyone, except me, went to the pub. (God knows why, since there must have been men there to contend with.) So much discussion about men's bestiality, so much emotion, so much earnestness, and so much real spite all delivered in a totally humourless way was a pathetic way to waste one's life I mused on the way home. And so it was a waste of my time getting involved in organizations which I did not believe were constructive or even useful. Perhaps I will have a go at Meals-on-Wheels next time I feel the doing-good urge – at least I know that is worthwhile.

My own theory on rape is that it is difficult to put the crime under one heading. There are many different kinds.

No one could possibly confused them. One is an outrageous attack on a woman, by a person or persons unknown. Another rape can be perpetrated by a husband, a son, a lover, or a family friend. For, I think, these men, when and if convicted, life imprisonment is too short. However, I have known of women both stupid and naïve in their dealings with men. In some cases, women invite men into their homes and lead them on with drinks and general coquetry and then are surprised and horrified when they are 'raped'. In my youth a crude saying "if you don't want the goods don't muck about with them" was expedient and, I think, still could be.

Attitudes eating out minus a male escort

On 28th March 1930, Vera Britten wrote a piece in the Manchester Guardian telling of her bizarre experiences when trying to buy a cup of tea of coffee in a public place, such as a restaurant or café, unaccompanied by a man, after a certain hour. She found it was not possible. The rules were made, presumably, with the thought that no woman without an escort after dark could be on legitimate business, such as wanting a cup of tea, but was obviously there solely to tempt men to prostitution. My own mother, in the thirties, before the divorce from her first husband was finalized, was courted by my father for many months without him being allowed to stay with her after 10 o'clock at night. There was a creepy fellow apparently called the Queen's Proctor, who, had he caught them at 10.01pm together, would have assumed they were having a sexual orgy. The inference being that sex could, or would, only take place after dark and after 10 o'clock. That was fifty years ago and since then some progress has been made, indeed the permissive society has been born. But there is still a long way to go it seems in changing the rules as to where unattended females are allowed, or dare, to tread.

A very old friend, Maggie, a painter from the North of Scotland and I decided, after a sad gap of several years, that we should meet somewhere for a weekend. York was agreed upon as a halfway house. We stayed at a lovely bed-and-breakfast farmhouse, just outside the city, but had to buy lunch and dinner elsewhere. On Saturday night Maggie suggested that we went somewhere special for dinner. We were recommended to go to a nearby hotel which had French food and was apparently very popular. So, we booked a table. We both dressed up in our best and I think we looked very respectable. The hotel car park was full of Mercedes, large Rovers, and sports cars. Despite high unemployment in the North, the old saying about 'where there is muck there is brass' seemed apt in that area, if nowhere else.

We walked into the restaurant to find flowers on every table, gleaming silver cutlery, lighted candles (of course) and linen napkins. The head waiter came up to us with a large smile. "Have you booked?" he asked. We told him we had. "A table for four?" he said. No, not a table for four, we said, for two. He looked puzzled. "For two?" he echoed our words. His smile vanished and a distinctly disapproving look came into his face. I suspect that the following kind of thoughts ran through his mind. (a) That he could say that there were no tables free so we would have to go elsewhere, or (b) that there would be a two or three hour wait until we would be served. But since we could see this was not to be so, he reluctantly showed us a table in the farthest corner of the room, as out of sight as possible.

Maggie, a married woman, had not really understood when I, newly single, told her briefly of the feeling of extreme vulnerability I had, as one of a minority group – like being single when convention and society mainly caters for doubles. Although we were a couple in this restaurant, we were both women. In a world where it is the norm for men to take women out to restaurants on a Saturday night, we were the *odd couple,* as it were. But although the waiter, when he finally materialized to take our order, did so with more than a touch of disdain, he could not spoil our enjoyment. Eventually the food arrived and it was delicious, we had interesting and lively conversation (not about men) and a good bottle of wine. Having a candlelit dinner with a woman friend is thoroughly to be recommended, with none of the complications of sexual domination or sexual attraction, or both. I do hope, as the sexes become more equal, women will be able to have lunch or dinner either by themselves or with another woman in an expensive restaurant without the feeling that they are unwanted outcasts intruding in an out-of-bounds no-go area. And, although we were allowed in the restaurant where I think it was unlikely anyone dining thought we were prostitutes, the attitude of the hotel staff had not, I thought, changed radically since Vera Britten's day.

The Tate Gallery

My daughter Jessica and I went on an outing to the Tate Gallery to see the Pre-Raphaelite Exhibition. An important point to this tale is that I am sufficiently old-fashioned and middle-aged to dress up when visiting our capital city, although studying the masses hurrying by, my assumption that others feel the same way I do, is misplaced. Those who went to the exhibition will remember the enormous crowds it attracted; more that 300 people every hour going through the rooms was the figure stated on the wireless. I had to queue so long to see the 'Light of the World' that Jessica was fed up and went off on her own. We were reunited about three hours later, spiritually fulfilled but bodily exhausted, hungry, and thirsty. We searched for the snack bar but long before we saw it, we saw the queue, four deep, going in its direction. We had little time left, and as I had seen a sign for the restaurant we decided to try there instead. Here there was no queue. A manageress approached us, looking us up and down. She said frostily: "This is the restaurant. The snack bar is down the passage." I told her of the queue, that I was in a hurry, and pointed out that I could read and knew therefore that I was in the restaurant, and that I wished to sit at a table for two people. "There is no table for two laid" she said, "Never mind, we are not fussy" I said, "we will sit at a table laid for four", and did so.

The restaurant was only half full and there were plenty of waiters standing about but it seemed that Jessica and I were invisible. We studied the menu and made up our minds. But no one came to take our order. A sort of silent pact seemed to have been made by the waiters: leave the old bag and daughter to stew. Eight young businessmen were sitting at the next table, guffawing, and swilling down bottles of chilled Sancerre. Indeed, they commanded a great deal of attention, but when I tried to catch the waiter's eye, somehow, he just did not see me. After half an hour we left. We bought sandwiches at a café down the road and ate them, reflecting, on a seat overlooking the Thames. Jessica was stoical but I was enraged. I asked myself these questions about expensive restaurant hostility to women:

> Are they worried women will not be able to pay the bill?
>
> Do women lower the standard of the restaurant by the lack of male escorts?
>
> Do women look like prostitutes?
>
> Do women understand the tipping system properly: 10% and all that.
>
> Do they think women will not buy wine which is how restaurants make their profits?

To these questions, I do not know, even yet, the answers. And probably never will.

Chapter 10

Summing up in 1982

Had I known of the many difficulties I had to face alone, I might never have started the journey. The easier choice is to stay within the security of marriage; however it might not be to your liking. Leaving it needs courage, determination, and a sense of humour because, indubitably, it is tough on your own. Especially so if you are over forty, not qualified for a well-paid job, (and not sure you would be capable of doing one, given the qualifications needed) and, in twenty odd years of marriage have been protected from the rates, the insurance and unwanted attention of visiting tradesmen.

To leave a marriage in the years after the dreaded fortieth birthday is a very different matter, I think, from returning to the single state in the twenties or thirties. The ineluctable truth is that after forty, your sexual attractions are considerably reduced. However, this is no disaster if solitude is the desired goal but this fact does make all the difference to the life to be led thereafter.

My sister, divorced and living alone in her early thirties, had more suitors than I could count. Going to stay with her in those days was lovely. She had a beautiful cottage in a valley under the Wiltshire downs. In the evenings sitting by a log fire, she told of romantic interludes in her own life with a variety of exciting men. The telephone rang constantly with calls from would-be suitors. She was very pretty and talented so it is not to be wondered at. I have known other women alone in their twenties or thirties who whirl about romantically with great success. But the demand for divorced women over forty is definitely less. Their romances are more usually to be nostalgically remembered than currently enjoyed. Obviously, I am not able to speak with authority for anyone save myself, but on evidence gathered from different sources (newspapers, magazines, novels and above all friends in similar circumstances) I feel, sadly, that my deductions are accurate.

In the first few single months I was in an emotional state. I felt extremely vulnerable, and wept a great deal. There were so many confusions and conflicts in my mind to think and worry about. Complete disorientation descended on me sometimes, to such an extent that I could not remember or think who I was, or what I was doing. It seemed that I was homeless, rootless, and lost. All day and much of the night I asked myself the questions about the failed marriage, over and over again. Friends at this time had to be very patient, and were, as I constantly repeated the same dreary things. Felicity was particularly kind while I stayed with her in the first week after my flight. Although very busy herself, she always made time to listen. And it is someone to listen that is needed more than anything else. I learnt to dismiss negative thoughts as a waste of time, and that whose fault it was or whatever, is simply a thought cul-de-sac. The decision to leave my marriage was not taken lightly or quickly. It is not a step anyone would take, I suspect, without great thought and deliberation. But, having made the decision, I had to believe that it was the right one. New and difficult roads had to be taken and all my strength needed for the forward journey. There was absolutely no time whatsoever for wasted energy looking back.

The first lesson I learnt was that I could only cope with each day as it came. Early on, very small things assumed very large proportions and if normal daily happenings for some reason failed, for instance the milkman forgetting to leave the milk, it seemed like a major disaster. But I am so glad that I learnt then about life on a daily basis. For me, it has proved the best way to live. I recommend reading Philip Larkin's poem 'Next, please'. In it he writes of the great importance of each single day. Before my metamorphosis, I literally wasted days. I let them slip by, unaware of their true value. Forgive me for repeating the pertinent old story about the octogenarian who, asked on his deathbed to elucidate on the good things he had done in his life, replied: "It is not the things I have done, it is the things I have not done that I mind about, and now I have no time." If I had continued the way I was going, smoking, and drinking too much, on an early deathbed I would have had only wasted years to look back on.

It is not that great things have to be achieved daily, I found, but I liked to try to achieve something daily however small, that earned my own self-respect. Something like ringing my mother, helping someone with something, or actually accomplishing in the day what I set myself to do, whatever it was. The importance of each day is highlighted in a prayer I particularly like by Professor William Barclay: "Help us ever to remember that we cannot tell if for us tomorrow will ever come." This is such an obvious truth, since we do not know what will happen to us any tomorrow, so I think if today has even a chance of being my last day, then it better be a good one.

Lesson Two was not only confined to being re-singled. Not only had I become single, but middle age had arrived as well. I had, reluctantly, to accept this fact from the amount of material evidence surrounding me. On the kitchen table sat cod liver oil capsules for stiff joints and approaching arthritis. I had acquired several pairs of spectacles – in the constant hope that one of them would be attractive – and my newest jacket was size 14. I had now to accept that the artistic director of life's theatre would no longer hand me out the lead parts. From now on, I thought, it is back row of the chorus – but it still took some time for this truth to sink in. Over the last year or two, seeing myself in mirrors or catching glimpses in shop windows, I had not accepted the reflected image. I would say to myself that the reason I looked such a fright was because I had a cold or some excuse, and replaced the image I wished to have of myself, back into my mind's eye. I suffered the age-old illusion of seeing myself as I wanted to be, rather than as I really was. I have often heard older people say that they feel no older inside than they did in their youth, and that they still picture themselves as young. This is a sentiment I have to agree with, though a small objective part of my mind reminds me that whatever I feel I still look – almost – my forty plus, years. Thomas Hardy, in his eighties, wrote a sad poem called "I look into My Glass." This is the last verse:

But Time, to make me grieve
Part steals, lets part abide
And shakes this fragile frame at eve
With throbbings of noontide.

I'm not, to be sure, eighty yet but I do know what he means. Indeed many poets lament about youthful feelings in ageing frames. Anyway, photographs, if enough are taken, do not lie. My friend Michael took some of me at a seaside resort we went to in the late summer, but it was still too hot for covering up in layers of shape-disguising clothes. The photographs, just like me, apparently, were not flattering. It was at this point I decided on a long-term diet: indeed, intermittent dieting has now become a way of life for me and, happily, the results are rewarding.

After considerable thought, I decided on a 'middle way' approach to my middle years. This was inspired by study of the Buddha who, after meditating for seven years, decided the best course to take in life was the 'middle way'. Not the hedonistic way, not the way of the ascetic, but something between. I did not wish to exercise myself for three hours a day in order to look seventeen again, or emulate Jane Fonda (whose ex-husband is alleged to have said that she is extremely boring as a result), nor did I wish to look matronly or mumsy. But it is possible to keep vaguely under eleven stone, and to buy clothes that don't look better on your daughter or your mother, and the importance of the effort is for yourself. If you live alone, it is essential to learn to like yourself, be your own best friend, since you are your only companion for many solitary hours.

Learning to live alone depends much on your attitude to doing so. If I had left my marriage in order to be with someone else, or if I anticipated a new partner to replace the one I had left, I would not have tried to learn about the joys of solitude. It is a commonly accepted fact that most people are lonely in their own company. They need someone to talk to, to share with, to confide in, or gossip to, and, to love. This is entirely natural since man is fashioned to have a mate, and it is considered odd to choose otherwise. I am genuinely happy on my own, whereas at gatherings of any kind I often feel lonely. Perhaps this is because I do not belong to any particular group. People like to belong to groups, or clubs, or classes, and feel safe when they are among their own kind. But loneliness is a difficult subject on which to elaborate with any authority, since it is a very personal matter. Where one might be lonely, another would not.

One thing I have learned from living on my own is that one's defences are constantly alert, for the solitary life is thought to be selfish. A harassed married friend staying with me one night said irritably "Well it's all right for you, no wonder you are happy, you live such a selfish life." If a selfish life is structuring the day as I please, choosing who I see and where I go, then, certainly, I do live a selfish life. But there are debits and credits to freedom. I have mentioned many of the credits. Here are some of the debits: the bills, the leaking roof, the quarrels with neighbours, or the constant fear after dark that perhaps tonight someone will break in. And other worries: if you fall and have an accident of any kind, and cannot telephone, who would know? Or care? How long would it be before someone came? Who would shop for you when you are in bed with flu? Who wants you for Christmas? These sorts of questions are vital to think about should you be thinking of a change.

The most important lesson of all was to learn to 'know myself'. To recognize my faults, to see myself as a reality, not as a fantasy, and to be my own judge and jury – 'mine own executioner'. I needed to find self-respect, we all do, since without it we despise ourselves and are in turn, despised. In Chapter 1 'know myself' was mentioned in a slightly defensive and pejorative way. But it is fourteen months since I started writing this book and I am now of the opinion that 'to know thyself' is the one important statement in it. My argument, to those sceptical, is this. If you start your life again, it has to have a new beginning. And the new beginning starts with you. And if you <u>do not</u> 'know yourself', do not understand your nature in the least, and have never questioned your attitudes or beliefs or why you have them, how on earth can you contemplate setting out? And if you do set out, without the vital knowledge of your own intricate workings, then success, I feel, is likely to elude you.

A subject constantly discussed is appearance and reality; nothing is what it seems. On that premise it is possible that you are not what you appear to be. Just because every year you take your annual holiday in Margate, or play golf on Sunday afternoons, or sit on committees, does not mean necessarily, that that is what you would wish to be doing, or even like doing. For years I sat as a magistrate. I sat on committees, and I sat at dinner tables where I discovered, on knowing myself, I did not wish to be in the least. I wrote a letter of resignation to the Lord Lieutenant, no longer sit on committees and I am no longer asked to fashionable dinner parties. The ensuing bliss is indescribable. It may cause merriment when I say "I found myself" since it sounds so ridiculous. But I did and risk being accused of foolishness by so declaring this. I like to think I am not self-satisfied or complacent as a consequence, since it is well-known that life is 'downhill all the way' after forty, and I will no doubt have my share of tumbles.

When unhappiness predominates your life, and you hasten ever faster and faster trying to chase elusive happiness, you observe nothing. But with the slower tempo of life suddenly ordinary things are viewed with a different eye, with a new sense of wonder and awareness. Driving slowly along the country lanes these days, the hedgerows tell me their seasonal stories. The first green buds, then the Flanders poppies and cow parsley, later the mistletoe and then the dark and bare branches of winter. I had never seen and thought about them before – just seen them, unaware.

I have often been asked how I knew I had made the correct decision to reapply for a single ticket. I did not know at the time of departure, but I know now. The man I married, and I were simply not in the least compatible. He likes rural pursuits and the touch of heather round his ankles and I like the touch of a pavement under my feet and a bus stop down the road. These are two fundamental differences where compromise is almost impossible. So, leaving was right for me. But each marriage is individual. Only you know how unfulfilled, unhappy, and unloved you are. And this could be your own fault. You could be unfulfilled because you do nothing, unloved because you are unlovable, and unhappy as a result of these two. To blame your partner for the misuse of your life is not justifiable. And leaving would solve nothing. But if, when thinking in the silence of the night, every aspect of your existence appears untenable, that the debit side is full, and the credit side is empty, then leaving it might be right for you. As it was for me. Obviously, there are problems and worries with any way of life, whatever it may be, shared or not shared and these last five years have not been easy. But I have found the peace I knew to be somewhere, and happy with it, I am very glad I made the break.

Many middle-aged women are supposed to seek consolation from religion. I suppose this means that, married or single, despairing of the human race, they turn to God as a last resort. The British as a race are inclined to shy away when God gets a serious mention: not many of them think of Him in terms of a possible strength, When talking about Him even in the vaguest terms, the facial expression of my friends leads me to believe that they think I have, finally, gone dotty. But for myself – and I suppose I am a middle-aged woman seeking consolation, I know that I could not have existed without God's support, guidance and most important, His Love, during this time. Therefore, I end this tale with a favourite quotation from Proverbs 15, Chapter 15: "He that is of a merry heart hath a continual feast." In my re-singled state, I have found this, unlike fallible human prophecies, to be one of solid truth.

Chapter 11

Two Michaels

[From this point, written forty years later in 2022.]

In the next four years one of the things I organized was a Poetry group in my house. Some very strange people came to it having seen the advertisement in the Oxford Library. One was a German student who didn't like my house or my old typewriter or my poetry, for that matter. Then there was an old man who had been a manager in the Ford Motor works, which was at the end of the Cowley Road. I don't really like poetry, he said, but I thought I would come along for the company. And there was a mad woman who never spoke and had to go outside for a cigarette every fifteen minutes. But it was fun and I think everyone enjoyed themselves in their own way. If nothing else they liked the coffee and biscuits and ate plenty during the evening.

During that time I went on Sundays to St.Barnabus' Church in North Oxford, which featured in Thomas Hardy's book, *Jude the Obscure.* This is why I chose it although it was very high church, with lots of incense floating about. It had a very bright ceiling as I remember it, blue with gold stars, which I liked looking at during the service. I became very friendly with the vicar, Father Michael, took me out to lunch sometimes and told me all the Oxford gossip. He was also a magistrate and we often sat on the bench together. Once he took me to an elegant dinner with a Japanese Prince and afterwards there was dancing and general gaiety.

Father Michael and I had many discussions about the Christian faith, never with very satisfactory answers from him. 'Why for instance' I asked him one day 'does God allow so much suffering in the world, so much injustice, so much greed, violence and intolerance. So many wars.' 'Ah' said Father Michael and then paused for a moment, thinking I suppose for a convincing answer, 'God moves in mysterious ways" he said finally, as if this was an entirely new idea. And that was about it. When I was a teenager we had the use of a small damp cottage with no electricity, and no mains water in North Norfolk. I very much wanted a pony and asked God to help me find one on many occasions. But He never did and eventually we were lent a small fat one called Joey, who came with a trap. I have often wondered why God doesn't intervene more in the ways of mankind. If He really loves us, as we are led to believe, He wouldn't want us to suffer as much as we do, or so I would have thought.

One Christmas Father Michael invited me to dinner in his house in North Oxford. There were two other priests there and a woman who I didn't know. During dinner the doorbell rang and I went to answer it. It was carol singers. I went back to tell Michael and he and his friends all said: 'Get rid of them for goodness sake'. I went to fetch my bag and gave them £2 of my own money. Not a very Christian action for priests I thought as I sat down. Then the strange part of the evening began. We went to sit in the sitting room and Michael found some tapes of music for us to listen to. The tapes were of Nazi marching songs, which kept the priests smiling, and at which they applauded. I felt very uncomfortable and left hurriedly. I wasn't asked again.

In 1978 I had been to a week's course on William Wordsworth's poetry in Kellogg House, Oxford, It was an interesting course but for the usual distraction. This time it was in the form of an Australian woman who liked to talk, interrupt, and tell us stories about her life which were nothing to do with Wordsworth's poetry. And the tutor didn't reprimand her; just let her talk on and on. I have found in the many courses I have attended on different subjects that there is always one student who monopolizes the class and seems totally unaware that it is not in order. And the tutors let them do it. And I suspect they let them do it because it is slightly less work than teaching.

Lucky for me that I went on this course because it was where I had met a scientist who worked for The Ministry of Defence. He was called Michael and became my faithful companion during those single six years. I never really discovered what exactly he did and I think I wasn't supposed to. One day the doorbell rang, I opened it and the caricature of an Englishman who reads the Telegraph, (he had one under his arm), was standing there. "Can I come in, I am Government Security, and need to speak to you", he said. We sat down and I poured some coffee for him, 'What is this all about?' I asked. It was about Michael. The sort of questions he asked me were: Did I know what Michael did when I wasn't with him? Was he gay, did I think? Did I know if he spoke Russian? I gave him the only information I knew and said tersely that of course I had no idea exactly what he did when I wasn't with him. I think the Ministry of Defence thought he was a spy and to this day I have no idea if they were right.

Michael was extremely clever, well read, and amusing. He was a rock for me in those turbulent years as a single woman in Oxford, and I will always be grateful to him for his constant support and, I think I can say, love. I can't really remember why we broke up but I think it was to do so with me wanting to be married again. I wanted a husband. I am not a woman who looks for a man with money to keep her, but for a constant legitimate loving companion, someone to call my own. And Michael was not the marrying type. So, for six months I was single again.

Chapter 12

Remarriage

I had been going to a writers' group in North Oxford run by a woman called Barbara Gordon Cumming. Barbara had herself written two novels; both published, and had two daughters who were authors too. We met once a month in different houses belonging to the group and I became very good friends with Barbara. One Christmas she invited me to a dinner party at her house and it was there I met Dr Geoffrey Ellis, an historian and my future husband.

At the dinner party there were some very officious women with very definite views on everything. We were discussing abortion and I said whatever one thinks about abortion it is, in my opinion, murder. This did not go down well.   The three women berated me, couldn't believe I thought that abortion was murder. I still think it is but if I were pregnant and didn't want the baby what would I do? Probably have an abortion even if I thought it was morally wrong to do so. Anyway, I sat next to Geoffrey and we had an interesting discussion about books and reading and I learnt that he was an historian and worked at an Oxford College. His wife and he were separated and he lived next door to Barbara. When I left the dinner party Geoffrey gave me a kiss on the cheek and said he hoped to see me again some time.

So, our romance began. I asked him to Warneford Road for dinner and invited Professor Norman Stone and his wife to come as well. The dinner was a great success and went on late into the evening.

After several outings to dine, to walk in the Botanical Gardens, to frequent pubs for lunch at the weekends, I met his boys, Robin and Jeremy. Robin was fifteen and Jeremy was eleven. The first time I met them they were really concerned, not about their parents' separation, but about the dog. They loved the dog but it had been impossible for Geoffrey's wife, Veronica, to look after him or for Geoffrey, since they both worked all day. They had found someone who could care for him, and take him for the walks he needed. I was a bit wary of the boys at first because having three girls of my own I didn't quite know how I should manage as a stepmother of boys. I found that boys and girls growing up are quite different species, but I think it worked well over the years that we shared a life and I grew extremely fond of them. I always thought of Jeremy as a kind of angel, he was so polite, studious and gentle. And he had beautiful red hair. But one day I took him with me to buy some party presents for something we were planning. The shop assistant was very unhelpful and hopeless and we left the shop empty-handed. 'Fucking stupid woman' Jeremy said and I was aghast. Could this beautiful boy have really said that? He was right of course but coming from him it was a revelation. We looked after the boys one week at a time and Veronica looked after them the other. It seemed to work very well, although maybe they would not agree with this assumption, looking back.

https://halfapairofpeople36.blogspot.com/p/chapter-12.htmlAfter five years of living together Geoffrey and I decided to marry.

We had a Registry Office wedding and then a Blessing in St. Michael's at the North Gate, Cornmarket Street, and a reception at my sister's house in Pullen's End, North Oxford. As a particular fan of Thomas Hardy, the writer, I decided that I would try to look like a Thomas Hardy bride. I am so hopeless at looking round shops that I asked my sister Angela to help me choose appropriate garments. We found a silk skirt in pale pink and a matching silk jacket; underneath I wore a white embroidery anglaise blouse with an ivory waistcoat and a pink tie. I wore a straw hat and did my hair in a small plait. My friend Felicity did say that I looked like a Thomas Hardy bride so I was very pleased. Geoffrey wore his only smart suit and gave a good and funny speech. He brought up that quote attributed to Oscar Wilde about a second marriage being more the triumph of hope over experience. So, I became a don's wife, rather different from being a don's secretary, which I was in Brasenose College Oxford some years ago. Geoffrey was a very hard worker and cared deeply about his students, but I had stipulated that I wanted a husband who would share some of the things that I wanted to do at the weekends and so I made him attend craft fairs, cinemas, pantomimes and lots of lunches in pubs. None of these things I think he did before he met me. My mother was very 'café' society of her time, she loved going to The Berkley Grill for lunch or to the Savoy or Claridges. Not quite the same as the local pub but where she liked to go to for fun. Perhaps this desire for restaurants and pubs is hereditary, because my idea of a lovely day out is to go to a country pub with delicious food and good company.

In case you are wondering, this is a short sketch of Geoffrey. He was small of stature with a clever, kind face and lots of beautiful soft blonde hair. He was very athletic and had played cricket for his college and squash to amuse himself. He was an historian and his specialist subject was Napoleon. Several of his books are published by OUP and have gone out all over the world. He had a very beautiful voice, which he used to sing whilst playing the guitar, and he often read the lessons in our church, St. Michael's at the North Gate. He was a very quiet and gentle man and much loved by many. I loved him very dearly for the thirty-one years we were together.

If you were a tutor at an Oxford College you were expected to dine at official dinners and eat at High Table. At quite some of these dinners I was invited as Geoffrey's wife. These occasions presented many difficulties for me. As I think you know by now, dear reader, I left school at 15 with three O levels and although I had tried to educate myself ever since, I had no degree to boast of or academic qualifications. Sitting between two rather fearful looking dons who inevitable asked me what my subject was, I was flummoxed. A feisty friend of mine equally married to a professor and with no degree was asked by a visiting don what her field was. 'My field?' she retorted. 'My field: I am not a horse.'. I was never rude, just puzzled at the strange behaviour of academics. In general, they seem unable to talk on any subject except their own with any interest, or perhaps they can't be bothered. The only don I enjoyed sitting next to was the English tutor because obviously we talked of our love of books, and I felt confident with him that

I knew what I was talking about for once. Although, of course, we could have talked about holidays, what children we had, the Government or anything else. But we didn't so I dreaded the dinners in college. Here is my last word about academics. They are a section of very clever men and women, who are unable to really connect with the rest of us. Geoffrey was an exception. When I worked in Brasenose College, I was the Fellows' secretary, which meant working for thirty dons, so I did know a disparate bunch. It is always difficult to generalize but during that year I soon learnt that dons live in a world of their own, immersed in their subject and not able to cope with much else, and nothing practical. But, as I said earlier in the book, they gave me very generous leaving presents, a kind card and I was sad to leave.

*   *   *

In 1984 I noticed that my right breast looked strange. The doctor however thought it was nothing but I was sure there was something wrong. Listening to the radio one morning I heard Jenni Murray say if you think you have something wrong with your breasts keep on trying to find out what it is. Right, I thought, I will. I went to see a consultant at the John Radcliffe Hospital in Oxford. I had a biopsy and was told that I had breast cancer. When I returned home that day Geoffrey asked me whether I would like a cup of tea. A cup of tea, I said, certainly not. I want a large gin and tonic. It was 10 am. I am sure that many people are like me when they learn that they have cancer, they can't really believe it. But I didn't have much time to think about it as I was summoned back to the hospital four days later for a full mastectomy. The night after the operation I thought about the part of my body that had I had lost and wept. I didn't want to have a reconstruction; more operations and pain were for me not an option. As I write this now at 82 years old, I have counted the operations I have had and they amount to seven. Four of them major so it is a wonder that I am here at all. From then on, I had to get used to wearing a prosthesis in my bra but otherwise life carried on as usual.

*   *   *

I have always loved poetry and decided to join a Creative Writing Class in Oxford. I had an enjoyable four years there and learnt a little about writing poetry. I have since discovered that poetry is not for everyone. Well, in fact, most people dislike poetry. If I said that I was a Christian who wrote poetry, at a party of any sort, I could empty the room. I had read somewhere that the Women's Institute were happy to enrol people for a performance at their meetings if you had something to say of interest or something to show. You had to have an audition, which terrified me, but I went and performed some of my poems. It was in a large Memorial Hall somewhere just outside Oxford. About thirty women were judging me as I stood on the stage trembling with fear. But I did it nevertheless and was suitably pleased with myself. Fortune favours the brave, I thought. A few weeks later I was telephoned and told I had passed and could start as soon as a WI branch wanted me. The telephone rang one day and we started being asked to perform. It was always exciting going somewhere new, each a hall had its own character, and a new group of women to meet. Between two or three of the poems Geoffrey played the guitar and sang. The Beatles songs were very popular and everyone joined in. All the women in the WI were so friendly and kind and we enjoyed ourselves immensely, sometimes weekly and sometimes every fortnight. But we had to carry the microphones and all the paraphernalia, my poetry books and Geoffrey's guitar across main roads, which was quite frightening and difficult. Then we started being asked to evening parties, which began at around 8.30. We tried to do this but it foxed us in the end. We couldn't always find the venue and arrived late and harassed. We were both in our seventies and it all was too much and after four years we sadly stopped doing it.

Chapter 13

Widowhood

In 2010 we were asked to a lunch party somewhere outside Oxford and it was there that Geoffrey first had difficulties with breathing and a heart pain. I rushed him back to Charlbury and telephoned the doctor. She confirmed that he was in trouble and booked a place straight away at the Manor Hospital in Oxford. He was in the hospital for a week having tests and finally given a stent. He was still working at the university and went back as soon as he could. But it was all too much for him and he retired; not as he would have wished but as I wished. He wasn't well enough to work. For the next seven years Geoffrey became less and less able in every way. He found walking difficult, slept in the afternoons and stopped writing a book he had wanted to finish. He had a crisis in 2017 and was rushed to intensive care in the John Radcliffe Hospital. He was there for three weeks and then my daughter Jessica very kindly fetched him and we brought him home.

He had become very small and very fragile. For the next three months I looked after him with the help of district nurses and physiotherapists. I made a bed up in the sitting room from where he could watch the television. Wimbledon was on at the time and he enjoyed watching the games. It was all very hard work and I was very tired. He couldn't really do anything without my help, which was lovingly given, and I truly thought he was getting better.

One Saturday we had been out for a picnic in the car, enjoyed ourselves, came back and he had a short sleep in the chair. I went upstairs to ring my daughter Eliza in the Cayman Islands. I next told him I would serve the supper at about seven. But very sadly when I came into the sitting room, I saw he had died in the chair. I was so shocked I thought my heart would stop beating. I rang our neighbours and Pete and his son Oliver rushed in and tried to resuscitate him, but to no avail. Jessica came over to help and to be with me. I was distraught. The worst thing I kept thinking of was that we hadn't said goodbye to each other. I hadn't told him how much I loved him that day.

Being a widow is horrific or at least it was for me. I hated every minute of it, I just couldn't become used to being on my own. Almost anything started a flood of tears sometimes two or three times a day. I have never had a group of friends who drop in at any moment and so frequently didn't see anyone for days at a time. Both my daughters Jessica and Tiffany were working and with all their commitments couldn't come to see me very much.

Somehow the weekends are the worst and Sunday is horrible on your own. Sunday is a very lonely day and was the worst day for me. I don't think people are generally meant to be solitary although, of course, some are quite happy on their own. Well, I wasn't one of them.

Those months after Geoffrey died were the worst times in all my life I had ever had and I watched myself heading for a nervous breakdown. Many unwanted thoughts came into my head especially in bed at night. What was the point of life now, was the sort of question I would ask myself? Would it matter to anyone if I wasn't here? There were many suggestions from family and friends that I might buy a dog. But much as I love dogs you can't have a good conversation with a dog and a dog is a big commitment, which I didn't feel up to. No. I decided I needed a companion to live with me and my granddaughter Emma provided the very solution.

Chapter 14

A Pair of People

One afternoon later in 2017, Emma my granddaughter came round for tea and told me her news. She had found a lovely man online with Tinder, the dating site. They had started going out and she was happy and excited. I had told Emma how very unhappy I was living on my own and she suggested that I went onto a dating site myself, obviously not Tinder which is for younger people but something suitable for my age.

I was quite reluctant to try this new form of meeting people but as it seemed to be the modern way, why not? I thought. I read The Telegraph newspaper, which had a dating site, and I decided that I would give it a try. You have to answer a multitude of questions before you start the procedure. This is a good idea because it gives any prospective suitor an idea of what you are like besides seeing your photograph. When asked what sort of person I would like to meet I put an academic. I had worked with academics, and been married to one for over thirty years and thought that I knew their foibles.

In mid-2018 I saw on my screen an academic who wanted to meet me. We started emailing each other, getting to know each other. I told him about my life and sorrow at being a widow, and he told me about some of his life and his sorrow at losing his wife after fifty years together. We then decided, two months later, to meet each other. But where? I suggested a pub in Burford, a town not far from where I live. A long way as it happens from his hometown of Ross on Wye. Still, that is where we met.

I arrived at the car park, got out of the car and saw at the entrance a tall man standing with his arms outstretched. I literally ran into them and he kissed me on my cheek. We held hands and walked into the pub. His name is Alan Francis Harrison, and is a retired professor. I love the name Francis, it makes me think of St. Francis of Assisi, my favourite saint, and Francis is the name we settled on straight away.

https://halfapairofpeople36.blogspot.com/p/chapter-14.htmlOver lunch, a waiter brought a big bunch of red roses to the table for me from Francis. It was so unexpected it brought a tear to my eye. After lunch he followed me back in his car to my house, which is in a small market town near Oxford. He brought his guitar from the car and played me two Flamenco pieces. Then we sat on the sofa and he kissed me.

What a surprise I had! I felt like a teenager all over again, brain a swirl and had difficulty standing up. Two weeks later he moved in and has been here ever since. He is perfect to live with, although I have to admit he is untidy. He looks after me at every turn. He is very amusing and we laugh throughout the day.

In mid-2018 I was diagnosed with lung cancer just three months after we had met. He came to the hospital every day and stayed with me, bringing food and comfort. After the operation, I didn't come round from the anaesthetic for over eight hours and Francis didn't leave my side. He was there when I eventually woke up. But I was discharged from the hospital too soon and so had complications with an infected abscess and had to return to hospital for two weeks on a drip of antibiotics. Francis again stayed with me every day. And when we arrived home, he spoiled me with tea in bed and lovely tempting lunches, flowers and cards.

I recovered slowly but without Francis I wonder how I would have managed? People have said he was heaven-sent and I believe there was some Higher Being involved. I think it is Jesus Christ who intervenes, as He has, I am quite sure, on many occasions in my life.

People have also said that I was brave to have tried computer dating. After all, I was 78 at the time I registered and perhaps should have known better. But for me the outcome was miraculous and still is.

We are both in our eighties now and have all sorts of aches and pains but we keep laughing and our life is very good. If you are single or a widow/widower reading this do be brave and give it a try. I know the newspapers are full of the terrible things that could happen to you finding someone this way, but I have two other friends who have been equally lucky in finding a loving companion doing computer dating with no problems. Just be sensible and careful. And good luck.

We live a very quiet life, which suits us. We eat well, exercise and when the weather is fair, we walk in the woods, breathe in the fresh air and listen to the birds. On return we have a glass of wine and a Roka biscuit. In the afternoon I have a nap then we watch the news at six. Francis makes the supper, usually two bowls of chicken soup and an apple. Then we play board-games and watch well-chosen films like Downton Abbey or Colditz. And we watch many films of the 1939/45 war, which we prefer to anything modern. Sometimes we ask friends to lunch or tea and we do like to go out to eat at an excellent nearby pub, on sunny days. All this may sound a little dreary to you but we are old now and it is just the right pace for us.

Epilogue

As we end our lives, we ask ourselves, don't we, how was it, our journey through, how did we do? Shakespeare said it all in his sonnet about the seven ages of man. Francis and I are now at the "sans everything' stage but hope for more years of good life together. I look back at my travels since childhood, into middle age, and now old age, and all things considered I have had a happy run. But I have also had lots of mountains to climb as I am an over-anxious person and that makes many difficulties living an ordinary, peaceful life.

I have had two cancer operations, one breast cancer, the other lung cancer, but I am still alive and eighty-two. I have three delightful daughters, Tiffany, Eliza and Jessica, plus four glorious grandchildren, all of whom have supported me in many ways over the years. I love them very dearly and know that they love me.

I have some very good old friends, one or two who I went to school with, and several I have known all my life. Those of us left and I have lost eight friends to cancer, keep in touch, talk and laugh together; sometimes on the telephone or on FaceTime. We have exceptionally nice neighbours who have been very supportive in lockdown, shopping for us or generally helping us with those things we can no longer do for ourselves. And they still do. And for the last nearly four years I have had Francis as my soulmate, my friend, and loving companion.

What have I learnt that may be useful to pass on to you? Simply this. That the Good Book and The Beatles know the truth about love. Love is patient, love is kind. It does not envy, it does not boast, it is not proud.

Love is all you need.

Acknowledgements

I thank Professor Francis Harrison (retired), my partner and editor, for all his help. His enthusiastic editing, I am sure avoided the book from appearing less deserving.

Thanks to Tiffany Watson and Jessica Deguera for their constant support of my blog and my poems.

Peter Moran has very kindly set the book ready for its availability on Amazon. Many thanks indeed! Thanks also to Nikki Moran for her wonderful and consistent kindness and support.

By the same author

Poems from Grace Cottage - 2006

More Poems from Grace Cottage - 2009

A Collection of Poems - 2016

The Ragbag of a Human Heart - 2019

Realisation – 2020

acotswoldpoet.blogspot.com includes most of my poems to date and updates relevant to the present book. Contact details therein.

Printed in Great Britain
by Amazon

81342774R00089